Projects *for* **Fiber Art Lovers**

COUNTRY COORDINATES TO QUILT, HOOK, STITCH, & PAINT

Contents

About *Rug Hooking* magazine **4**
and *The Quilter* Magazine

From the Editors **5**

CHAPTER 1
PRECIOUS PANSIES **6**

Precious Pansies Quilted Banner **8**
by Barbara Campbell

Precious Pansies **15**
Penny Rug Table Mat
by Jacqui Clarkson

CHAPTER 2
HERE A CHICK, ...**20**
THERE A CHICK

Here a Chick, There a Chick
Hooked Rug **22**
by Barbara Carroll

Here a Chick, There a Chick
Penny Rug **27**
by Wendy Thomas Walsh

CHAPTER 3
COUNTRY COTTAGE **36**

Country Cottage Queen-size Quilt **38**
by Michele Crawford

Country Cottage Canvas
Floorcloth **44**
by Colleen Rundgren

CHAPTER 4
RED BIRD **48**

Red Bird Hooked Rug **50**
by Alice Strebel and Sally Korte

Red Bird Wool Quilt **53**
by Alice Strebel and Sally Korte

CHAPTER 7
CHRISTMAS STAR 86

Christmas Star Lap Quilt 88
by Mark Lipinski

Christmas Star Table Runner 92
by Mark Lipinski

Christmas Star Pillow Pair 95
by Mark Lipinski

Christmas Star Ornaments 98
by Mark Lipinski

Christmas Star Cross Stitch 100
by Mark Lipinski

General Rug Hooking Directions 103

General Quilting Directions 105

Rug Hooking Resources 108

CHAPTER 5
FRUIT THEOREM 62

Fruit Theorem Painting 64
by Nancy Rosier

Fruit Theorem Hooked Rug 69
by Sheri Bennett

CHAPTER 6
PUMPKINS IN THE ROUND . . .74

Pumpkins in the Round
Hooked Rug 76
by Jenny Rupp and Lisa Yeago

Pumpkins in the Round
Penny Rug 80
by Jenny Rupp and Lisa Yeago

About RUG HOOKING *Magazine*

*R*ug Hooking magazine, the publisher of *Projects for Fiber Artist Lovers*, welcomes you to the rug hooking community. Since 1989 *Rug Hooking* has served thousands of rug hookers around the world with its instructional, illustrated articles on dyeing, designing, color planning, hooking techniques, and more. Each issue of the magazine contains color photographs of beautiful rugs old and new, profiles of teachers, designers, and fellow rug hookers, and announcements of workshops, exhibits, and gatherings.

Rug Hooking has responded to its readers' demands for more inspiration and information by establishing an inviting, informative website at www.rughooking online.com and by publishing a number of books on this fiber art. Along with how-to pattern books, *Rug Hooking* has produced the competition-based book series *A Celebration of Hand-Hooked Rugs*, now in its 16th year.

The hand-hooked rugs you'll see in *A Celebration of Hand-Hooked Rugs XVI* represent just a fragment of the incredible art that is being produced today by women and men of all ages. For more information on rug hooking and *Rug Hooking* magazine, call or write us at the address on page 5.

About THE QUILTER MAGAZINE

*T*he Quilter Magazine is a pattern magazine for quilters of all skill levels. Each issue contains a variety of pieced and appliquéd projects ranging from full bed-size quilts to small lap quilts, wall hangings, and table settings. The projects are photographed in styled settings to convey scale and to provide decorating and design ideas. Every project is accompanied by a source of supply, so that readers can, if they wish, mail order the exact fabrics that are featured in the magazine. In addition to patterns, *The Quilter* also contains features of interest to readers, including articles about top designers, travel destinations, quilt show exhibits, sewing collectibles, and antique quilts. You can find *The Quilter* at book and craft stores, quilt shops, and at large chain stores nationwide.

EDITORS

Virginia P. Stimmel, *Rug Hooking* Magazine

Laurette Koserowski, *The Quilter Magazine*

MANAGING EDITOR

Judy P. Sopronyi

BOOK DESIGNER

CW Design Solutions, Inc.

ASSISTANT EDITOR

Lisa McMullen

PHOTOGRAPHY

Impact Xpozures

CHAIRMAN

M. David Detweiler

PUBLISHER

J. Richard Noel

Presented by

R·U·G
HOOKING

1300 Market St., Suite 202 • Lemoyne, PA 17043-1420

(717) 234-5091 • (800) 233-9055

www.rughookingonline.com • rughook@paonline.com

in cooperation with

The **Quilter** Magazine

7 Waterloo Rd. • Stanhope, NJ 07874

(973) 347-6900 • (800) 940-6593

www.thequiltermag.com • editors@thequiltermag.com

PLEASE NOTE: All patterns and finished pieces presented here are Copyright© the individual designers, who are named in the corresponding chapters. No finished piece presented here may be duplicated for commercial purposes in any form without the designer's consent. No warranty or guaranteed results are implied in the instructions. Personal skill and materials used will affect the results. Stackpole, Inc. does not assume responsibility for injuries, damage, or other losses that result from the material in this book.

PRINTED IN CHINA

Contents Copyright© 2006. All rights reserved. Reproduction in whole or in part without the written consent of the publisher is prohibited.

Canadian GST #R137954772.

From the Editors

During the past several years, fiber arts have enjoyed unprecedented growth and recognition in all areas—quilting, hooked rugs, coverlets, and penny rugs, to name just a few. Exhibits at well-known museums, such as the American Folk Art Museum in New York City and the Quilt and Textile Museum in Lancaster, Pennsylvania, frequently feature antique and contemporary quilts, hooked rugs, woven coverlets, and floorcloths—utilitarian items used by our ancestors as necessities that are now viewed as works of art. These same items are often sold at the finer craft shows throughout the country, and one needs only to visit commercial quilt shops to find that rug hooking patterns and wools have found a place beside the quilting materials.

Based on the growing interest in learning how to make these wonderful fiber art projects, and in further wanting to expand our energies into the creative market, *Rug Hooking* magazine and *The Quilter Magazine* are excited to present our first joint project together, *Projects for Fiber Art Lovers: Country Coordinates to Quilt, Hook, Stitch, and Paint.* The book represents a blend of coordinated projects, each designed to be made in at least two different ways using the same pattern elements—such as a pattern for a quilted banner and a penny rug mat, or a painted theorem and a hooked rug. The combinations are intriguing, and we have even included two seasonal projects for Halloween and Christmas. *Projects for Fiber Art Lovers* contains projects to appeal to everyone from the beginner to the advanced level.

If you have a "can do" attitude and are looking to develop your artistic talents, this beautifully illustrated book will be your guide to expanding your creative horizons. Written in an easy-to-read format, each chapter of *Projects for Fiber Art Lovers* will make you want to begin your project today. Which one to start first will be the hardest decision. Have fun and remember the sky is the limit!

—The Editors:

Ginny Stimmel, *Editor,*
Rug Hooking magazine
Laurette Koserowski, *Editor,*
The Quilter Magazine

Laurette Koserowski

Ginny Stimmel

Precious Pansies

These two delightful projects share the same pattern pieces and can be embroidered either by hand or machine. The appliqué pieces on the banner are fused and machine embroidered using straight, buttonhole, and zigzag stitching. The penny rug, also fused, uses a variety of hand-embroidered stitches.

Precious Pansies Quilted Banner

BY BARBARA CAMPBELL

INTERMEDIATE
Finished quilt size:
17½" x 50½"
Finished block size:
10" square

MATERIALS

- One 8" square each of wavy stripe fabric (for umbrella) and yellow fabric (for flower centers)
- One 10" square each of two different pink, one dark green, and three different purple fabrics (for flowers and leaves)
- ⅓ yard of maroon print fabric (for baskets and umbrella handle)
- ⅜ yard of medium green print fabric (for block backgrounds, buds, and leaves)
- ⅝ yard of light green tonal fabric (for leaves and setting triangles)
- ⅝ yard of mottled purple fabric (for basket, umbrella, sashing, and binding)
- 22" x 56" piece of batting
- 22" x 56" piece of backing fabric
- Thread in colors to match fabrics (for piecing and quilting)
- 1½ yards of double-sided fusible web
- Cardboard or clear template plastic
- Non-stick pressing sheet (or parchment paper)
- Water-soluble or tear-away stabilizer
- Basic sewing and embroidery supplies

CUTTING

From the maroon print fabric, cut:

- One 10" square (for basket bottom)
- Reserve remainder for basket rim and umbrella handle appliqués

From the medium green print fabric, cut:

- One 12" x 42" strip; recut into three 12" squares
- Reserve remainder for leaf and bud appliqués

From the light green print fabric, cut:

- One 18¼" square; cut diagonally in half twice (for side setting triangles)
- Two 9⅜" squares; cut diagonally in half once (for corner triangles)
- Reserve remainder for leaf appliqués

From the mottled purple fabric, cut:

- Four 2¼" x 42" strips (for binding)
- One 10" square (for basket bottom)
- Six 1½" x 12½" strips (for sashing)
- Six 1½" x 10½" strips (for sashing)
- Reserve remainder for umbrella appliqué

BLOCK ASSEMBLY

1. *Preparing the appliqués.* Using the pattern pieces provided, trace the outside edges of the appliqué shapes onto cardboard or template plastic and cut out. Retrace all the shapes (except the basket bottom) onto the paper side of the fusible web. Trace one umbrella, two basket rims, and enough flowers, buds, and leaves to recreate the look of the featured project. Roughly cut out each shape. Following manufacturer's directions, fuse the traced flowers to the wrong side of the pink and purple fabrics and the bud and leaf shapes to the wrong side of the dark green and light green fabrics. Fuse the basket rims and umbrella handle to the wrong side of the maroon fabric. Fuse the outside of the umbrella to the wavy stripe, and fuse the inside of the umbrella to a piece of mottled purple. Cut out neatly on the traced lines and set aside. Fuse a piece of web to the back of the 8" yellow square. Trace and cut enough small flower centers for all the pansies.

2. *Woven baskets.* Trace one basket bottom on cardboard or template plastic. Cut two 10" squares from the fusible web. Fuse the web to the wrong side of each maroon print and mottled purple 10" square; cut eleven $3/4$"-wide strips from each square, then re-cut six strips in half. Remove the paper backing. Place the five longer maroon strips horizontally, right side up, on the non-stick pressing sheet and pin the ends on one side to hold in place. Alternately weave the shorter strips vertically between the pinned strips (see **Diagram 1**). When satisfied with the woven fabric panel, press to fuse in place. Remove from the ironing surface and use the template to cut the basket bottom shape. Repeat with the mottled purple strips.

3. *Appliquéing the blocks.* Place the three 12" medium green squares on point. Remove the paper backing from the appliqué pieces prepared in Step 1. Referring to the photograph and beginning with the bottom pieces, arrange the baskets and rims, umbrella, flowers (without centers), and leaves on the squares, centering each overall design. When satisfied with the arrangement, fuse in place. **Note:** *The blocks will be trimmed to $10^{1}/_{2}$" square after the machine stitching is finished, so be sure to leave enough room around the entire arrangement.*

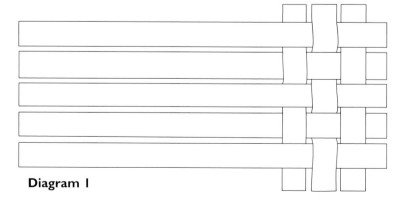

Diagram 1

DECORATIVE STITCHING

Note: *All stitching was done free motion and with feed dogs dropped on the sewing machine. If your machine doesn't have that capability, you can tape an index card over the feed dogs.*

1. Following manufacturer's instructions, pin stabilizer behind each block to avoid puckering while stitching. With matching thread, satin stitch the stems on each flower using a short stitch length and long stitch width. Buttonhole stitch around the outside edges of the flowers and basket pieces. Use small zigzag stitches to highlight the basket weave and flower petals and straight stitches to add decorative details to the petals and leaves.

2. After all the flower details are embroidered, fuse the yellow centers in place.

3. Remove the stabilizer according to the manufacturer's directions. Keeping the design centered, trim the blocks to $10^{1}/_{2}$" square.

Barbara Campbell is a professional quilt designer from Pine Brook, New Jersey, whose patterns have been published in several different quilting publications including The Quilter *and* Fabric Trends. *Barbara also designs sample quilts for fabric manufacturers and has her own pattern business. You can learn more about Barbara by visiting her web site at www.loveinstitches.com.*

BANNER ASSEMBLY AND FINISHING

1. **Sashing strips.** Stitch the $1^{1}/_{2}$" x $10^{1}/_{2}$" mottled purple strips to two opposite sides of the embroidered blocks. Press seams toward the purple fabric. Sew the $1^{1}/_{2}$" x $12^{1}/_{2}$" strips to the remaining sides of the blocks, again pressing strips toward the purple fabric.

2. Following the **Banner Layout Diagram** on page 12, stitch the light green side setting triangles and corner triangles to the blocks, creating diagonal rows as shown. Sew the rows together, aligning the points of the blocks. Trim the banner top evenly to $^{1}/_{4}$" past the block corners.

3. Layer the backing (right side down), batting, and banner top (right side up). Baste the layers together and quilt as desired. **Note:** *The featured project was quilted in the ditch around the sashing strips and around all the motifs in the basket blocks. The setting triangles were quilted with a butterfly motif.*

4. Stitch the four $2^{1}/_{4}$" x 42" strips, short ends together, into one long binding strip. Fold the strip in half with wrong sides facing. With raw edges aligned and leaving a 6" tail, sew the strip to the top of the banner through all layers, mitering the corners and overlapping the ends. Turn binding to back of banner and hand-stitch in place.

QUILTED BANNER AND PENNY RUG TEMPLATES

Banner Layout Diagram

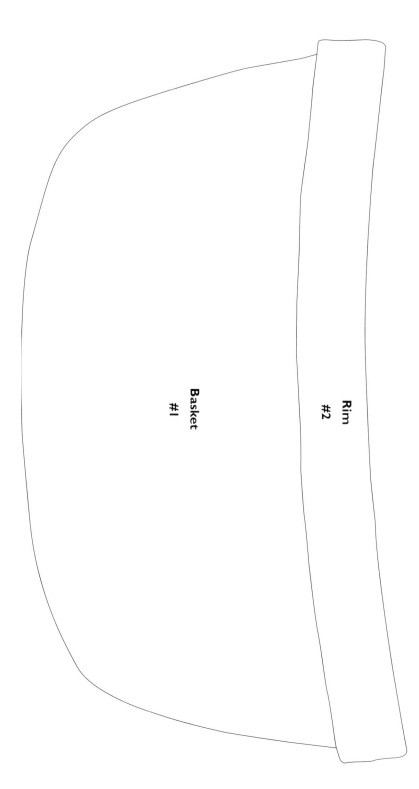

Basket
#1

Rim
#2

#1	Basket	#8	Large Leaf
#2	Basket Rim	#9	Small Leaf
#3	Large Pansy	#10	Large Butterfly
#4	Medium Pansy	#11	Small Butterfly
#5	Small Pansy	#15	Large Bud Base
#6	Large Bud	#16	Small Bud Base
#7	Small Bud		

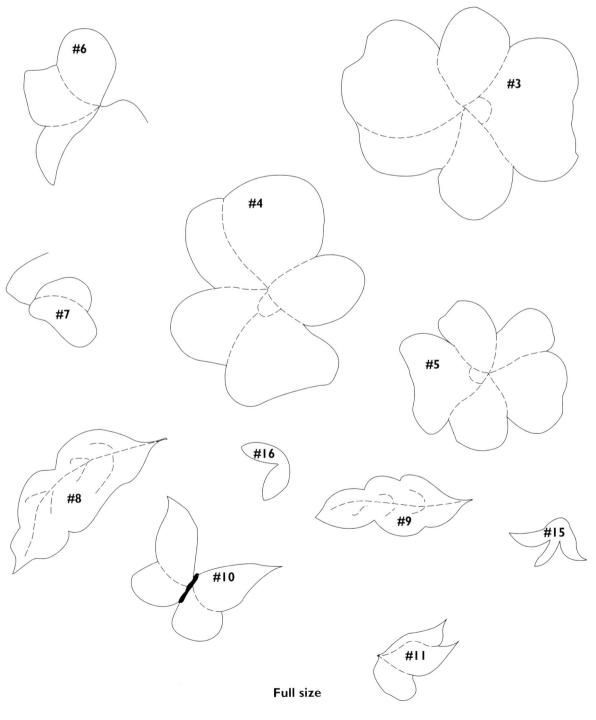

Full size

#12	Umbrella Top
#13	Umbrella Handle
#14	Umbrella Bottom

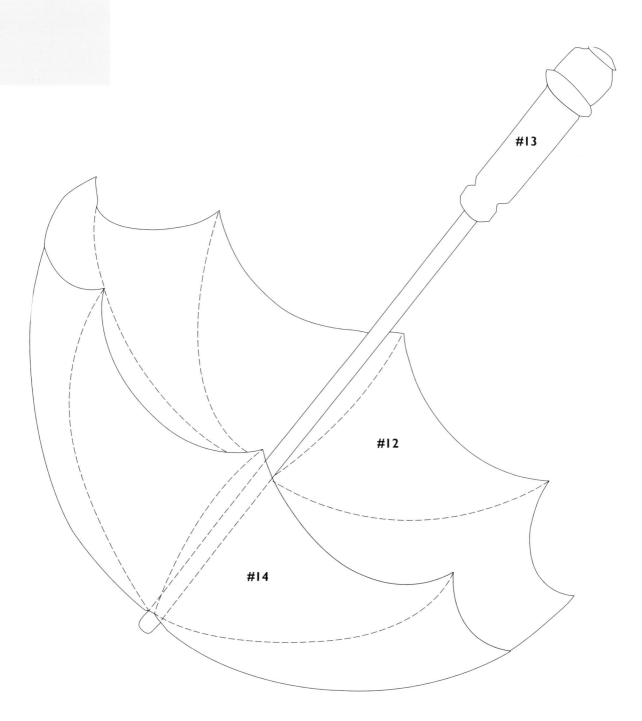

Full size

Precious Pansies
Penny Rug Table Mat

BY JACQUI CLARKSON

MATERIALS

- $^1/_2$ yard of spring green wool (for penny rug background and lambs' tails)
- Eleven 10" wool squares in the following colors: purple tweed (for basket), blue (for butterflies and lambs' tails), two different greens (for leaves), three different pinks and four different purples (for flowers)
- Scrap of yellow wool (for centers of pansies)
- Hand embroidery needle and perle cotton size #8 in medium pink, light pink, purple, green shade of leaves, green to match background fabric, pale yellow green, bright yellow, and blue
- $^1/_2$ yard of cotton backing fabric
- 1 yard of double-sided fusible web
- Cardboard or template plastic
- Non-stick pressing sheet or parchment paper

CUTTING

1. Trace the oval background, lambs' tail templates, and appliqué patterns onto cardboard or template plastic and cut out. Use the background template to cut one oval piece from the spring green wool. Also cut four lambs' tails using Template A and 12 lambs' tails using Template B. Using the half penny pattern, cut sixteen pennies from the assorted pink, blue, and purple wool pieces.

2. Prepare the basket by fusing a 10" purple tweed square to a 10" square of fusible web. Cut the fused square into eleven $^3/_4$"-wide strips. Save the remainder of the fabric for the basket rim. Cut six of the $^3/_4$"-wide strips in half. Remove the paper backing and pin the longer strips on one end to a non-stick pressing sheet. Using **Diagram 1** on page 10 as a guide, weave the shorter strips vertically between the longer ones. Press to fuse in place. Make one template for the basket bottom (page 12) and one for the rim. Using the templates, trace and cut the bottom from the woven piece and the rim from the leftover fabric.

ASSEMBLY

1. Referring to the photo for placement, center the woven basket on the background fabric (approximately on the bottom third). Fuse in place, remove the paper backing, then fuse the rim to the top of the basket. With matching perle cotton, buttonhole stitch around all outside edges of the basket and rim.

2. Using the photograph as a guide, arrange the pansies and leaves on the background. When satisfied with the arrangement, pin in place. Make sure that the ends of the leaves are tucked under the flowers.

3. Beginning with one flower and leaf arrangement, set aside the flower, then buttonhole stitch around the outside of the leaf with matching perle cotton. Use a fly stitch for the veins in the leaf centers.

Place the flower on top of the leaf, and buttonhole stitch around the edges with matching perle cotton. Use stem stitches between the petals for definition and to create detail lines (three to five lines) on each petal.

4. When stitching the buds, use a buttonhole stitch around the edges and a stem stitch for petal definition. Use lazy daisy stitches at the base to create small leaves. **Note:** *Try placing two or three lazy daisy stitches on top of each other so that they appear full when surrounding the buds.* To create the stems, stem stitch two rows side by side and then weave the thread around both rows to create a "whipped" look.

5. Place the two butterflies last, so they appear to be approaching the basket of pansies. Buttonhole stitch around the wings and use stem stitching for definition. Create the bodies by making two lazy daisy stitches—a larger one for the bottom of the butterfly's body and a smaller one for its head. Again, you may wish to place several lazy daisy stitches on top of each other for a fuller look. Finish with a small stem stitch for the antennae and a small French knot for the knob.

6. Cut little triangles of yellow wool to place in the center of each pansy. Stitch into place with a small running stitch.

7. Place the four pointed lambs' tails (cut from Template A) in the middle of each side edge of the oval background piece and pin in place on the back of the fabric. Pin three shapes (cut from Template B) between each of the four pointed pieces, spacing them as evenly as possible.

8. Pin the assorted penny half-circles on top of the tails. Remove each tail, one at a time, then buttonhole stitch the circles on with coordinating perle cotton. Pin the tails back in place, about $1/2$" below the edge of the background piece. Buttonhole stitch each tail onto the background fabric, as well as around the outside edge.

9. Press the wrong side of the backing fabric on the fusible web and use the oval template to trace and cut the shape. Remove the paper backing and fuse with the right side facing out onto the back of the embroidered piece to finish. **Note:** *It is not necessary to back the lambs' tails.*

Jacqui Clarkson is a thread and fiber artist/teacher who has taught at cross-stitch festivals, trade shows, the Embroiderers' Guild of America, and at national seminars of the American Needlepoint Guild. She has written numerous articles for magazines. Her commissions have included oversized ornaments for the Christmas tree in the Blue Room of the White House and needlework pieces in support of World Aids Day. Jacqui can be contacted at jacquindle@aol.com.

STITCH KEY

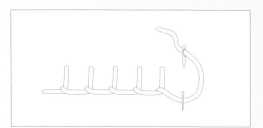

BUTTONHOLE STITCH

Working from left to right and holding the thread down with your thumb, make a downward vertical stitch. Bring the needle over the thread and pull into place.

FLY STITCH

Come up with the needle at point A and go down at point B. Hold the thread in a loop and bring the needle up at point C, below the midway point between A and B. Loop the thread under the needle and draw through gently. Anchor with a long or short stitch.

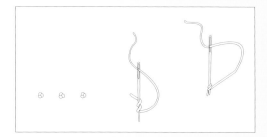

FRENCH KNOT

Bring the needle up and circle the thread twice around the needle. Holding the thread off to one side, insert the needle in the fabric as close to the starting point as possible. Hold the knot in place until the needle is pulled through.

LAZY DAISY

Bring the needle up from the back of the fabric and hold the thread flat with your thumb at point A. Insert the needle at the starting point so that the thread forms a loop. Bring the needle out a short distance away so that the needle passes over the thread. Make a small anchor stitch at the top of the loop.

RUNNING STITCH

This stitch is the same as the quilting stitch. Working from right to left, make small even stitches that are the same length as the spaces.

STEM STITCH

This stitch is worked from left to right. Sew along the designated line keeping thread to the left of the needle. Come up in the center and the right side of the previous stitch.

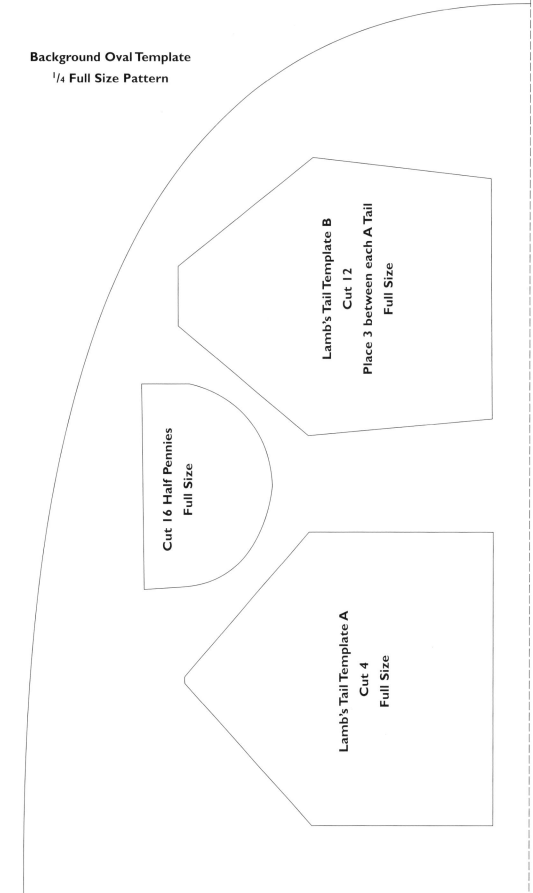

Background Oval Template
¹/₄ Full Size Pattern

Lamb's Tail Template B
Cut 12
Place 3 between each A Tail
Full Size

Cut 16 Half Pennies
Full Size

Lamb's Tail Template A
Cut 4
Full Size

Flip and Trace

Flip and Trace

Here A Chick, There A Chick

These projects share an animal theme, with animals that would have been part of family life as pets or livestock. Both designs were worked in a dark color scheme with a definite "make do" feeling due to the use of scraps that were on hand, much like our ancestors might have done. Some of the colors are similar in value, where others provide striking contrast and add liveliness and interest to each piece.

A light or even a "fantasy" color scheme would work equally well for this design. Many old quilts have animals in unnatural colors, which would only add to the pieces' charm.

Here A Chick, There
A Chick Hooked Rug

by Barbara Carroll

©2005 Woolley Fox LLC Rug Design

MATERIALS

- Monk's cloth backing 27" x 30"
- 1$^1/_4$" binding tape 121"

Wool quantities below are calculated at six times the size of the motif or area to be hooked. If you hook low you will need less, and if you hook high you will need more.

- **Dog**—a few miscellaneous strips for the eye, nose, mouth, and the outline of the ear. For the body of the dog, the total amount of wool you will need is 22" x 23". If you use three different wools, cut three pieces of wool about 8" x 22".
- **Horse**—a few miscellaneous strips for the eye, mane, and the hoofs. For the body of the horse, the total amount of wool you will need is 20" x 21". If you use three different wools, cut three pieces of wool about 7" x 20".
- **Rooster**—a few miscellaneous strips for the comb, wattle, beak, eye, outline of the wing, and the fill of the wing. For the body of the rooster, the total amount of wool you will need is 14" square. If you use two wools in the rooster, cut two pieces about 7" x 14".
- **Cat**—a few miscellaneous strips for the eyes, nose, and mouth. For the body of the cat, the total amount of wool you will need is 16" square. If you use two different wools, cut two pieces about 8" x 16".
- **Chicks**—a few miscellaneous strips for the eyes. For the body of the chicks, the total amount you will need is 16" square. If you use four different wools, cut four pieces 4" x 16".
- **Corners**—several miscellaneous strips for the curved stripes.
- **Background**—the total amount of wool that you will need is one yard. If you use six different darks, cut six pieces 10" x 36".

INSTRUCTIONS

I had so many leftover dark strips of wool that I thought it would be fun to hook using all of those and not cutting any new wools for the background.

1. The dog and the horse are definitely the focal point of this rug. Decide their colors first. Then, as you hook the cat and the rooster, it will be easier to choose their colors.

2. Start with the dog. Hook his eye, nose, and mouth first. Outline his ear (I used a darker wool for the outline) and then fill in the ear, hooking in the shape of the ear. The same wool was used for the fill of the ear that was used on the outline of the dog. Now hook the outline of the dog, making sure that you hook just inside the line. Complete the dog next. I used three different wools to fill the body following the shape of the dog, but then

created some "spot" areas with the wools. Have fun—this is a big dog and you can play with your wools.

3. Again for the horse I chose three wools. The outline of the horse was hooked first, and I just used whatever wool came up. So the outline is not just one wool. Hook the mane next using six different colors of wool. Now hook the eye. Fill the body next. Cut the three different wools and hook them in however you pull them out of the pile of strips for the horse. Also, you might want to hook in a lighter strip or two in the end of the horse's tail. Hook the hoofs next—it is a bit hard to see, but I hooked three of the hoofs using the same wool and one front hoof a bit different.

4. Hook the rooster next. Because the dog and horse are sort of "quiet," I thought this was the time to "pop" things up. So why not a rust rooster? And, of course, a teal comb and wattle! I outlined the entire rooster with one sort of "specky" rust and also filled in the feet with the same wool. Hook the eye now. For the wing, a soft gold wool was hooked just outside the line for the wing, then a second outline of the darker red, and the wing was filled in with a nifty red/camel herringbone. This makes the wing "quietly" interesting. Use the darker red and soft

gold in the tail also. Now fill in the rooster with your rooster wool. I used just one wool to fill in the rooster. Hook the comb, wattle, and beak next.

5. Now for the cat—red seemed like it would "pop" the rug up, and it's bold enough to hold up against all of the chicks. The rust rooster also helps anchor the chicks. I chose to use only one wool to outline the cat; make sure that you stay just inside the line. Hook the eyes, nose, and mouth next. Here I thought a quiet wool would be best. Only two reds were used to fill in the cat, but you could definitely use more. A bit of the outline wool was also used to hook a defining line in the cat's tail.

6. For all of those chicks, use lots and lots of different golds, and for the eyes just use "brightish" wools. For some I hooked in a wing, and for others I didn't. I also used only one gold per chick—outline, fill, and the feet. So, if you have four different golds—A, B, C, D—then use A for some chicks, B for some chicks, etc. Make sure to hook just inside the line to outline the chicks so they don't "billow" up.

7. I hooked in my background as I hooked in the chicks. If you choose to do this, make sure that you hook one row of background wools on the outside line of the rug. This will contain your hooking—

sort of like outlining the animals.

8. For the background, as I mentioned, I used all of my leftover dark wool strips. If you do not have that many, then choose about five or six dark wools and cut them up and randomly pull up a strip to hook the background or use a wonderful dark plaid with lots of muted colors in it. I played with my background by creating different lines of wools in some of the areas. There is no right or wrong here—outline all of the animals, then just hook in your background wools.

9. The nifty corner is next. In order to contain the hooking, I hooked one line on the outside line of the pattern by using the different wools I was using in the corners. So hook a line of the taupe, then pick up the teal and hook that, then the wonderful red/camel herringbone, the gold, and finally the deep red—go around the corner and start back up with the colors in the order they should be in. Now just hook in the areas of color by hooking on the curve and from one side to the other. I used only the colors in the rug (no, you do not need to do this) and made sure that no reds touched the cat.

FINISHING

See page 103 for finishing instructions.

Barbara Carroll is the author of The Secrets of Primitive Hooked Rugs *published by* Rug Hooking *magazine. Her work has also appeared in several issues of* Rug Hooking *magazine and in* A Celebration of Hand-Hooked Rugs II *and* III, *the 1992 and 1993 editions of the annual book produced by* Rug Hooking. *Barbara lives with her family in Ligonier, Pennsylvania.*

The pattern should be enlarged to 22¹/₂" x 26" for use (approximately 325%)

Here A Chick, There A Chick Penny Rug

BY WENDY THOMAS WALSH

To create a penny rug in a suitable size for a table or wall, I reduced the templates on a copy machine, but not uniformly. Inspired by an old "story" quilt with an animal theme and in keeping with a folk art feeling, the animals are in disproportionate size to one another.

MATERIALS

Wool:

- 17¹/₂" x 21" piece of wool for background
- 17¹/₂" x 21" piece of black wool for backing
- 12" x 15" piece of background wool for tongues
- 12" x 15" piece of black wool for tongue backing
- 10" x 10" piece of plaid wool for top of tongues
- 10" x 8" piece of wool for dog
- 7" x 7" piece of wool for rooster's body
- Scraps for rooster's crown and wattle
- 10" x 7" piece of wool for horse
- Scrap of brown wool for horse's hoofs
- 7" x 7" piece of wool for cat
- Scraps of light and dark gold wools, textured and solid, for chicks
- Scraps for large, medium, and small pennies

Flosses:

- 5 skeins DMC #310 Black
- Light and dark gold flosses to match wool for chicks and their wings
- Light blue for some of the chicks' eyes

Other:

- Various colors of wool roving or yarn for animals' features
- 38-gauge star point and 40-gauge finishing hand felting needles
- Block of upholstery foam for felting base
- Freezer paper and Sharpie® marker
- Light box (optional, for tracing)
- Large eye tapestry or chenille needle
- Sharp appliqué scissors

INSTRUCTIONS

1. Trace the four main animal shapes onto freezer paper with the marker. If you have one, a light box is a great tool for tracing. Trace on the dull side of the freezer paper. *Note: Where dashed lines are drawn on pattern pieces for the rooster's crown and wattle and the horse's hoofs, this indicates that those pieces should be cut down to the dashed line. This is the area that will be overlapped by the main body pieces.*

2. With the freezer paper's shiny side down, iron the traced piece onto the wool for each shape. Cut shapes out with sharp appliqué scissors.

3. Position the four main animal shapes where desired on the background piece and pin in place.

4. Using three strands of black floss, blanket stitch (see page 82) the four animals in place. Overlap the rooster's crown and wattle and the horse's hoofs as indicated on the pattern pieces.

5. Trace and cut as many chicks as you want from a mixture of gold wool scraps using the three different chick motifs. This penny

Needle Felting

Needle felting, or "dry felting" as it is also called, is actually a relatively new craft. It was only back in the early 1980s that fiber artists began working with the small, sharp, barbed needles used by woolen mills to produce commercial felt for their hand-felted creations. It is rapidly growing in popularity among artisans, crafters, and doll makers.

The needles used for hand felting today are very thin and wickedly sharp with barbed tips that can break easily. During the hand felting process the fibers of the wool roving or yarn are "married" to the base material with the repetitive process of stabbing into it with the felting needle. These needles come in various sizes for various degrees of felting from coarse to fine, and the sharp ends are usually triangle shaped. A needle with a star-shaped end is also available. It allows for faster and finer work and better resistance to breakage. I used a star-shaped needle for the initial felting, following up with a triangle-shaped needle for finer finishing of the felted area. Typically a block of upholstery foam is used as a base on which to work.

Begin by selecting the smallest wisp of fiber. Position it where desired and use your needle to make random stabs into the fiber to "baste" it to your background. Then needle the fiber to the background by repeatedly stabbing into it, gently pulling the fiber into the shape you want with the tip of the needle or a toothpick—not your finger! Pick up your work often to prevent it from sticking to the foam.

Wool roving (cleaned, carded wool fiber) is the most common choice for hand felting and is becoming more widely available. Fibers pulled from wool yarns can also be used if you cannot find roving in the colors you want.

Needle felting is a very forgiving craft—if you don't like the way your felted area looks, it can be pulled right out for a "do over"! Have fun, experiment, but remember to keep those fingers out of harm's way!

---

rug has a dozen chicks, but you could do more or less. Reverse some of them for interest.

6. Scatter the chicks around the background, arranging them the way you like. Pin the chicks in place.

7. Appliqué the chicks in place using two strands of matching gold floss and a small primitive stitch.

8. With the various flosses, make French knots (page 18) for the chicks' eyes. Use three strands of floss and wrap the floss around the needle four times to make a nice eye.

9. With three strands of contrasting gold floss, give each chick a wing with two long stitches.

10. Using the three different penny templates, trace and cut three-layer or two-layer pennies. Blanket stitch (page 82) top pennies to the bottom pennies, then blanket stitch the completed penny units to the background.

11. Needle felt the animal's facial features as described in the box above. Refer to the pattern pieces to see where the felting should be done.

12. Using several colors of wool roving, needle felt the horse's mane.

13. Using light gray roving, needle felt the cat's eyes, nose, and mouth.

14. Using dark brown roving, needle felt the dog's nose, eye, and ear outline.

15. Using dark gold or yellow roving, needle felt the rooster's beak.

16. Using black or dark gray roving, needle felt the rooster and horse eyes.

17. Again using the freezer paper, trace and cut out eight large tongues from the background wool.

18. Trace and cut out eight large tongues from the black wool.

19. Trace and cut out eight smaller tongues from the plaid wool.

20. Blanket stitch the plaid tongues atop the large tongues using three strands of black floss.

21. Layer the completed top tongue units to the black background tongues and blanket stitch all around using three strands of black floss.

22. Place completed penny rug top, face up, on black background piece and pin together.

23. Slip tongues between top and bottom pieces approximately $3/4"$ inside the rug "sandwich," spacing them equally. Pin securely in place.

24. With four strands of black floss, blanket stitch all around penny rug. When you come to the tongues, stitch into the top layer of wool only. The tongues will be secured from the back later.

25. After stitching all the way around the rug, flip over to the back and blanket stitch the undersides of the tongues, being careful to only stitch through the black wool.

You might want to whipstitch a simple label on the back of your wonderful creation with your name, the date, and any other information you'd like to add.

Wendy Thomas Walsh has been quilting and enjoying other needle arts for about ten years. More recently she has developed a passion for working with wool, including dyeing, rug hooking, and penny rugs. Wendy has turned her love of folk art and primitives into a successful on-line business, Simple Folk, www.simplefolk.com, specializing in the folk art and primitive designs she loves.

TEMPLATES FOR HERE A CHICK, THERE A CHICK PENNY RUG

(All line drawings are full size)

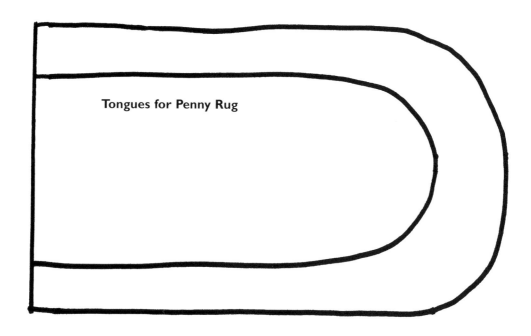

Tongues for Penny Rug

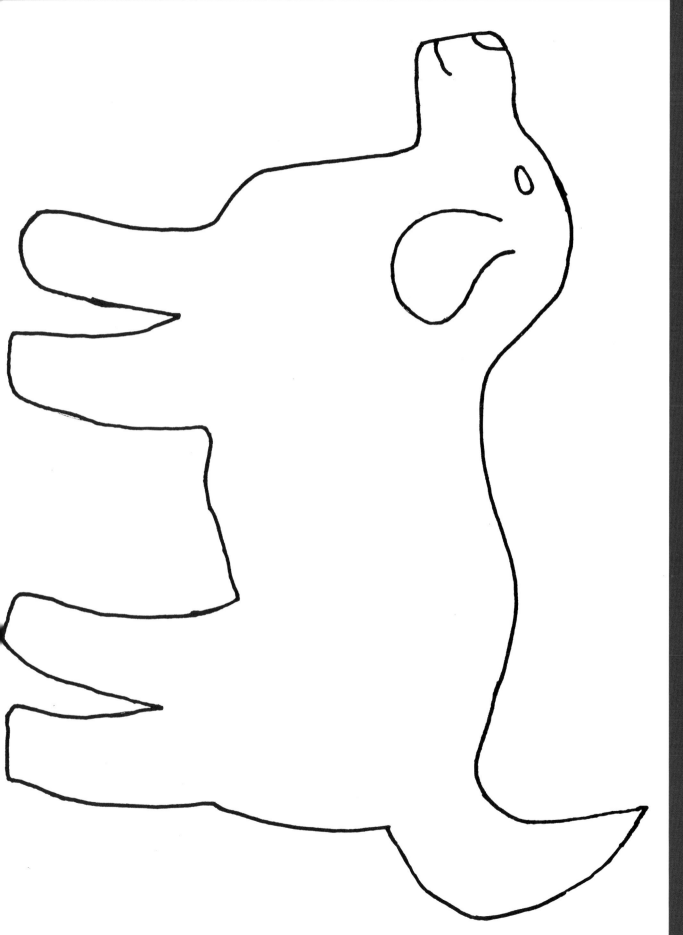

Pennies
for Penny
Rug

Country Cottage

Michele Crawford used a Four Points block design, in two different color combinations, to make this stunning traditional queen-size quilt. For a truly coordinated look, Colleen Rundgren stenciled a canvas floorcloth with acrylic paints in colors to match the fabrics.

Country Cottage Queen-size Quilt

BY MICHELE CRAWFORD

Finished quilt size:
87" x 99"
Finished block size:
12" x 12"
Number of blocks:
30
(15 Block A
15 Block B)

MATERIALS

Yardage is based on 42"-wide cotton print fabric designed by Lynette Jensen of Thimbleberries for RJR Fabrics (www.rjrfabrics.com).

- $1/2$ yard of medium burgundy fabric
- $1/2$ yard of pink floral fabric
- $3/4$ yard of medium green fabric
- $3/4$ yard of dark burgundy fabric
- $3/4$ yard of olive green fabric
- $1^7/8$ yards of cream fabric
- $2^1/4$ yards of medium blue fabric
- $3^3/4$ yards of light blue floral fabric (includes binding)
- 91" x 103" piece of backing fabric
- 91" x 103" piece of batting
- Sewing thread in cream, blue, and green
- Machine quilting thread in cream
- Rotary cutter, ruler, and mat (optional)
- Cardboard or plastic template material
- Basic sewing supplies

CUTTING

From the cream fabric, cut:
- Eleven $3^3/4$" x 42" strips; re-cut into one hundred twenty $3^3/4$" squares, then cut diagonally in half once (Piece 1)
- Seven $2^1/2$" x 42" strips (for first border)

From the medium burgundy fabric, cut:
- Seven 2" x 42" strips (for second border)

From the pink floral fabric, cut:
- Four $2^3/8$" x 42" strips; re-cut into sixty $2^3/8$" squares (for Block A)

From the medium green fabric, cut:
- Four $5^1/4$" x 42" strips; re-cut into sixty $2^3/8$" x $5^1/4$" pieces (for Block A)

From the dark burgundy fabric, cut:
- Four $5^1/4$" x 42" strips; re-cut into sixty $2^3/8$" x $5^1/4$" pieces (for Block B)

From the olive green fabric, cut:
- Four $2^3/8$" x 42" strips; re-cut into sixty $2^3/8$" squares (for Block B)
- Eight $1^1/2$" x 42" strips (for third border)

From the medium blue fabric, cut:
- Fifteen $3^1/2$" x 42" strips, then cut into 120 of Piece 2. **Note:** *The pattern for Piece 2 is shown on page 40 and includes a $1/4$" seam allowance. Make a template from the plastic or cardboard, then cut the number of pieces indicated.*
- Eight $2^1/2$" x 42" strips (for fourth border)

From the light blue floral fabric, cut:
- Four $2^1/2$" x $99^1/2$" lengthwise strips (for binding)
- Two $7^1/2$" x $99^1/2$" lengthwise strips (for fifth side border)
- Two $7^1/2$" x $73^1/2$" lengthwise strips (for fifth top and bottom border)
- Thirty $5^1/4$" squares with floral motif centered (for Block A and Block B centers)

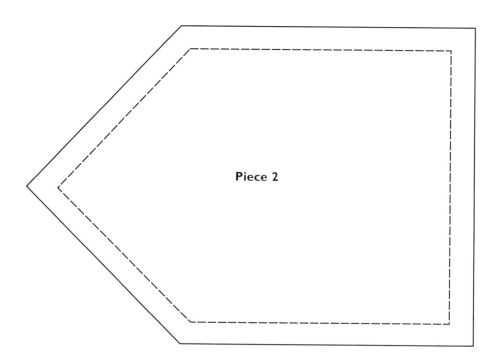

Piece 2

DIRECTIONS

Use a ¹/₄" seam allowance throughout. Sew all pieces with right sides together and raw edges even, using matching thread. Press seams toward the darker fabric after sewing each piece.

Block A Assembly

1. Following **Diagram 1**, sew a cream Piece 1 to each long side of a blue Piece 2. Repeat to make a total of four units. Trim evenly.

2. Referring to **Diagram 2**, stitch a medium green piece to opposite sides of a 5¹/₄" light blue floral square. Sew a pink floral square to each end of two additional medium green pieces, then stitch these units to the top and bottom of the block center. The unit should measure 9" x 9".

3. Following the **Block A Diagrams**, sew the units made in Step 1 to each side of the units made in Step 2 to assemble one 12¹/₂" x 12¹/₂" block.

4. Repeat Steps 1 through 3 to make a total of 15 blocks.

Block B Assembly

1. Following **Diagram 1**, sew a cream Piece 1 to each long side of a blue Piece 2. Repeat to make a total of four units. Trim evenly.

2. Referring to **Diagram 3**, stitch a dark burgundy piece to opposite sides of a 5¹/₄" light blue floral square. Sew an olive green square to each end of two additional dark burgundy pieces, then stitch these units to the top and bottom of the block center. The unit should measure 9" x 9".

3. Following the **Block B Diagrams** on page 42, sew the units made in Step 1 to each side of the units made in Step 2 to assemble one 12¹/₂" x 12¹/₂" block.

4. Repeat Steps 1 through 3 to make a total of 15 blocks.

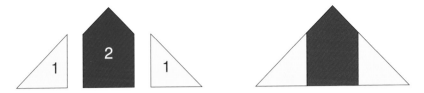

Diagram 1

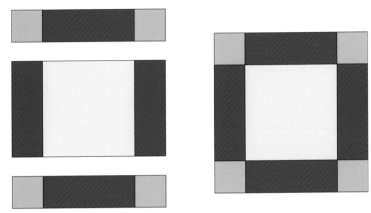

Diagram 2

Block A Diagrams

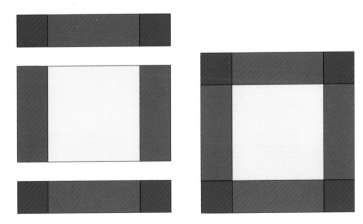

Diagram 3

Quilt Assembly and Finishing

1. Referring to the **Quilt Layout Diagram** on page 43, sew the blocks alternately together into six horizontal rows of five blocks each. Press the row seams in opposing directions. Stitch the rows together to complete the $60^{1}/_{2}$" x $72^{1}/_{2}$" quilt center.

2. *First border.* Sew the seven $2^{1}/_{2}$" x 42" cream strips, short ends together, into one long strip. Press seams open. Cut into two $60^{1}/_{2}$" strips and two $76^{1}/_{2}$" strips. Stitch the shorter strips to the top and bottom of the quilt center. Press. Sew the longer strips to the sides. Press.

3. *Second border.* Stitch the seven 2" x 42" medium burgundy strips, short ends together, into one long strip. Press seams

open. Cut into two $64^{1}/_{2}$" strips and two $79^{1}/_{2}$" strips. Sew the shorter strips to the top and bottom of the quilt top. Press. Stitch the longer strips to the sides. Press.

4. *Third border.* Sew the eight $1^{1}/_{2}$" x 42" olive green strips, short ends together, into one long strip. Press seams open. Cut into two $67^{1}/_{2}$" strips and two $81^{1}/_{2}$" strips. Stitch the shorter strips to the top and bottom of the quilt top. Press. Sew the longer strips to the sides. Press.

5. *Fourth border.* Stitch the eight $2^{1}/_{2}$" x 42" medium blue strips, short ends together, into one long strip. Press seams open. Cut into two $69^{1}/_{2}$" strips and two $85^{1}/_{2}$" strips. Sew the shorter

Block B Diagrams

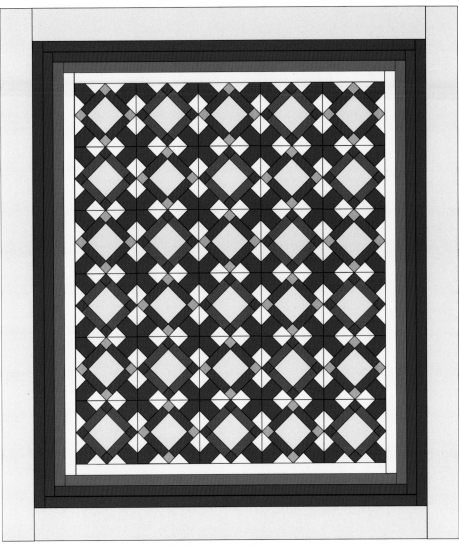

Quilt Layout Diagram

strips to the top and bottom of the quilt top. Press. Stitch the longer strips to the sides. Press.

6. **Fifth border.** Sew the 7^1/$_2$" x 73^1/$_2$" light blue floral strips to the top and bottom of the quilt top. Press. Stitch the 7^1/$_2$" x 99^1/$_2$" strips to the sides. Press.

7. Layer the backing right side down, batting, and quilt top right side up. Baste the layers together. Quilt as desired. (The featured project was quilted in an overall continuous line motif.) Trim backing and batting even with quilt top.

8. Sew the light blue floral strips into one long strip and bind the quilt edge as desired. (See General Quilting Directions, page 105, for help.)

Michele Crawford of Spokane, Washington, has been a freelance quilt and needlework designer for 16 years. She has had more than 4,000 quilting and sewing designs published in a variety of craft and needlework publications. Many of her quilts have been displayed at various national and international trade shows. To purchase more of Michele's patterns and kits, visit www.flowerboxquilts.com.

Country Cottage
Canvas Floorcloth

by Colleen Rundgren

AMERICAN TRADITIONAL DESIGNS®

MATERIALS

- 2' x 3' primed canvas floorcloth by Fredrix®*
- *American Traditional Designs*® stencils: Antique Rose (#CS-32), Berry Vine with Hearts (#BL-582), and Triple Border (#BL-31)** (patterns on page 47)
- *American Traditional Designs*® stencil brushes: $5/8$" #SA-102, $3/8$" #SA-100, $1/4$" #SA-001**
- Assorted foam brushes
- Acrylic paints: medium dark red, periwinkle blue, cream, black plum, dark green, yellow ochre, and golden brown
- Water-based polyurethane varnish
- Low-tack tape
- Yardstick or ruler
- Pencil
- Paper towels
- Spray sealer

Available at most art supply and craft stores.
**Available at most craft stores or visit www.americantraditional.com or call (800) 448-6656.*

DIRECTIONS

1. Apply a base coat of cream paint to the floorcloth. Apply a second coat to ensure coverage. Set aside to dry.

2. Using a pencil, measure and lightly mark a borderline all the way around the floor-cloth, $3/4$" away from the outside edge. Measure and mark a second borderline $4^1/4$" away from the first border, crossing lines at the corners to create four squares. Measure and mark a third borderline $1/4$" away from the second, leaving a large center rectangle.

3. Place low-tack tape along the outside edge of the third borderline. Paint the center rectangle with a wash of periwinkle blue thinned with water, allowing some of the base color to show through. Allow to dry and repeat until desired coverage is achieved. Remove tape when dry.

4. Place tape around the outer edges of the corner squares and, with a wash of dark green, paint them in a "slip-slap" motion to create a textured look. Allow to dry and repeat until desired coverage is achieved. Remove tape when dry.

5. Place tape around the outer edges of the wide border rectangles and paint with a wash of medium dark red. Allow to dry and repeat to obtain desired coverage. Remove tape when dry.

6. Use tape to mask the hearts of the Berry Vine with Hearts stencil. Center the stencil at one end of a red rectangle and tape in place to secure. Stencil with black plum. Remove the stencil and repeat to complete the background vine design in each red rectangle.

Tips & Suggestions

- Use low-tack tape to mask areas of the design to be left unpainted, or use it to create crisp edges for stripes and borders.
- Use very little paint on the brush. Tap the brush bristles in the paint and wipe the excess onto a paper towel with a swirling motion. The swirling motion helps to evenly distribute the paint on the bristles. Pounce or swirl the paint from the solid part of the stencil toward the openings. A darker tone is achieved by either adding more pressure to the brush or by adding another layer of paint.
- Begin stenciling with the lightest color. Add the next darker color, blending it with the first color in some areas to create a variety of tones. Continue in this manner until the desired result is achieved.
- Use one brush per color to avoid muddying the final design.
- Do a "practice run" to become familiar with the design and to decide what colors and shading are desired.
- Try creating a custom-sized or -shaped floorcloth by cutting and priming your own canvas with several coats of gesso.
- Use a minimum of three to five coats of varnish for durability and easy cleanup. This floorcloth can be wiped clean with a damp sponge.

7. Position the tulip motif as desired and secure with tape. Add cream to medium dark red and dark green to create lighter shades of both. Stencil the tulip design using these blended colors. Remove the stencil and repeat to create a random "calico" pattern.

8. Position the Antique Rose design on the center rectangle, referring to the photograph as a guide. Following the Tips & Suggestions above, and referring to the photo for color placement and highlighting, stencil the Antique Rose design using cream, medium dark red, dark green, and yellow ochre. Repeat to create a random "fabric" look.

9. Allow the floorcloth to dry completely. Spray with sealer to set.

10. Create a wash of golden brown paint thinned with water. Randomly apply the wash to the floorcloth with a wide foam brush. Use a paper towel to wipe off the excess "wash" to create an antiqued look.

11. Following manufacturer's directions, apply three to five coats of varnish.

Colleen Rundgren is a professional painter and designer for American Traditional Designs, which specializes in home décor and paper crafting products. Visit www.americantraditional.com to see a whole gallery of ideas by Colleen and other American Traditional designers.

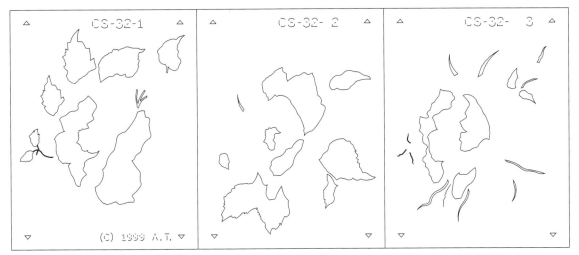

CS-32-1   CS-32- 2   CS-32- 3

(C) 1999 A.T.

Antique Rose—enlarge 200%

Berry Vine With Flowers—enlarge 200%

Tulip—Full Size

Red Bird

The idea for the color scheme and design was inspired by the charming old quilts we've collected over the years. The colors are subtle, and the motifs are simple. The Bird-on-a-Tree motif is found in many of the old quilts.

For this quilt and rug design, just as it is in our lives, it was hard to stay uncluttered and plain. Why is that? We are always attracted to the simple pieces but find those the most difficult to design. In the end we did resist the temptation to add more of everything and are very pleased with the final results.

The red trim around each of the tongues on the quilt and the red border on the hooked rug rescue the pieces from blandness.

We used the same motifs and all the same wool in both the quilt and rug, and as a result they look great together.

Red Bird Hooked Rug

BY ALICE STREBEL AND SALLY KORTE

MATERIALS*

All yardages are 54" wide unless otherwise indicated.

- One yard each of a medium taupe, a darker taupe, and a charcoal/black wool
- One 17" x 20" piece of red wool
- $^1/_2$ yard of dark brown wool
- One 8" x 17" piece of gold wool
- One 20" x 68" piece of linen rug hooking foundation fabric
- Heavy red wool yarn for binding
- A length of jute or a slim cord that will go around the perimeter of the rug for binding
- A large needle with a blunt tip and an eye large enough to hold the yarn
- A primitive hook

* Hand-dyed wool in the red, gold, and green; red, charcoal, and taupe wool threads; 100% chunky wool yarn in red; Fun Finishes booklet on how to finish rugs by The Potted Pear; and all manner of rug hooking supplies are available online at www.kindredspiritsdesigns.com.

DIRECTIONS

The rug is hooked in a #8 ($^1/_4$") cut.

1. First draw the design on the linen backing. Start by drawing an 11" x 60" rectangle. Next divide this shape into seven smaller rectangles. The rectangles on each end that feature the tongues measure 5". The other five rectangles all measure 10".

2. Divide the center rectangle in half from corner to corner, forming two triangles. Divide one of these triangles into five strips of different widths. Beginning with the strip in the center, the strip widths measure 1$^1/_4$", the next strip is 2" wide,

then 1", next 1 3/4", and the last strip is whatever space remains in the corner.

3. Transfer the motifs onto the foundation fabric. Also trace three tongues on the last rectangle at each end of the rug. Since the design motifs are so simple, we suggest that you cut out the patterns (pages 58-61) and trace the shapes onto the background.

4. In order to later cut and bind the scalloped shape at each end of the rug, sew on top of the trace lines for the tongues. This will keep the linen backing from fraying when you cut around each tongue.

5. For the outline around the star, cut a few gold strips in a #6 (3/16") cut. Cut the rest of the wool that is for hooking into #8 (1/4") strips.

6. Hook the birds in red. Hook the trees and the star in charcoal. The star is outlined with the narrower gold strips.

7. Next hook the tongues. One tongue on each end is hooked in brown, one in charcoal, and one in gray. Hook a single gold row in the middle of each tongue.

8. Hook the background spaces. The rectangles that contain the bird are hooked in the darker taupe, and the rectangle with the tree is hooked in the lighter taupe. The solid part of the triangle in the center is hooked in brown. The strips on the other half of the center triangle can be hooked in any of the background colors you wish.

9. As the finishing touch, bind the rug with the red yarn. The binding technique we used on this rug is one of our favorites and is published in a Potted Pear book on

finishing techniques. To prepare the rug for finishing, cut away the excess backing from around the rug, leaving about 1 1/2". You may wish to machine-sew along the edge to keep it from raveling. Lay the jute or cord along the edge and roll the backing toward the hooking, right up to the hooked edge. The jute will be inside the roll like the lead inside a pencil. We prefer to baste this rolled edge in place before we begin the binding. Next thread the needle with the yarn and "whip" the yarn around the rolled edge, covering it completely as you move along.

Red Bird Wool Quilt

BY ALICE STREBEL AND SALLY KORTE

Finished size:
2' × 3'

MATERIALS*

All yardages are 54" wide unless otherwise indicated.

- $1/2$ yard each of light taupe, dark taupe, and dark brown wool
- $3/4$ yard of charcoal/black wool
- $1/3$ yard of gray wool
- 1 square yard of any color wool for the back of the quilt
- $2/3$ yard red wool
- 8" × 12" piece of gold wool
- $1/3$ yard of green wool
- 36" square piece of thin cotton batting
- Strong red thread or floss
- Charcoal, gold, and taupe wool thread

* *Hand-dyed wool in the red, gold, and green; red, charcoal, and taupe wool threads; and 100% chunky wool yarn in red are available online at www.kindredspiritsdesigns.com.*

CUTTING

- Cut two 12" × 12" squares each of light and dark taupe wool.
- Cut one 12" × 12" square each of brown and charcoal wool.
- Cut out a pattern for a right triangle whose sides measure $12^1/2$" × $12^1/2$" × $17^1/4$". Use the pattern to cut out one gray, one brown, and one dark taupe wool triangle.
- To make the fabric for the pieced blocks, cut 26"-long strips of the following colors and widths and sew them together:

- — one 2" brown strip
- — one 3" brown strip
- — one $2^1/2$" dark taupe strip
- — one $2^3/4$" dark taupe strip
- — one $2^1/4$" light taupe strip
- — one 3" gray strip
- — three $2^1/2$" light taupe strips
- Using the tongue pattern provided, cut out the following tongues:
  - — eight brown
  - — six charcoal
  - — five gray
  - — nine mixed taupes
- Cut twenty-eight 2" × 13" bias strips from the red wool to go around each tongue.
- Cut one red bird and two red flowers.
- Cut four gold circles and sixteen gold flower tips.
- Cut two flower stems with the red flower tops and two stems with the gold flower tops.
- Cut one charcoal tree and three stars.

Red Bird Dye Formula

- $1/2$ tsp ProChem Chinese Red
- $1/2$ tsp ProChem Brick Red

over one yard of Dorr camel wool

1. Put the dye in a one-cup measure. Add one cup boiling water and stir well so all the dye dissolves.
2. Add the dye solution to a large pot that contains the wool and enough hot water so it is about 3" higher than the wool.
3. Stir well and often to get an even distribution of dye.
5. After about 15 minutes, add 1 tablespoon citric acid crystal or $1/4$ cup vinegar.
6. Stir occasionally and allow the water to barely simmer for 30 to 40 minutes until all the dye is absorbed.
7. Allow to cool, then rinse and dry. You can rinse and dry in the washer and dryer.

DIRECTIONS

1. First build the background of the quilt on which the appliqués will be placed. The background consists of nine blocks. Six of the blocks are one solid piece of fabric, and the other three blocks are pieced. Sew everything with $1/4$" seams and right sides together.
2. To prepare the three blocks that are pieced and split in half on the diagonal, first sew all the wool strips together to make a piece of fabric that is 26" long. From this strip of fabric cut three triangles using the pattern you constructed. Refer to the photo to decide the direction you want the stripes to go on your triangles.
3. Place each wool triangle you just cut out on the solid wool triangles. Sew together across the longest side, creating a square.
4. Next lay out all the background squares and corresponding appliqué pieces to see that all is going as planned.
5. Sew the appliqués to the background with one strand of wool thread, using either a whipstitch or a buttonhole stitch (page 18). The four flower appliqués are centered in the middle of their background blocks. The three stars are stitched onto the solid area of the three pieced blocks. The tree and bird lie across two background blocks. To do the tree and bird, you must first sew those two blocks together. The tree is sewn on with taupe thread, the stars with gold, and the rest with charcoal.
6. When all the appliqués are done, assemble the front of the quilt by machine sewing the nine blocks together. Next feather stitch (see next page) all the seam lines with the charcoal wool thread.
7. Lay the quilt top on the backing fabric and cut the backing fabric the same size as the quilt top. Do the same thing with the cotton batting. Remove the quilt top.
8. Next, prepare the twenty-eight tongues. Sew the bias strips to the tongues with slightly less than a $1/2$" seam. Sew the right side of the bias strips to the right side of

the tongues. Roll the bias to the back of the tongues and press. To finish, hand stitch the bias to the back of the tongues. As you stitch, roll the raw edge under as little as possible to get a nice clean look.

9. Pin the tongues in place on the quilt top. Pin seven tongues to each side with all the straight edges of the tongues even with the edge of the quilt top. The tongues should be evenly placed along the side, and you must leave a $^1/4"$ seam allowance at each end of each side. You may have to ease in some of the tongues to get them to fit. This fullness should iron out.

10. Baste all the tongues in place around the background.

11. To assemble the quilt, place the front and back right sides together, then place the batting on the backing. Pin all together. Leaving an opening along one side to turn the quilt right-side out, sew all the way around the quilt. Press and stitch the opening closed.

12. The last step is to tie the quilt. We used a strong red thread and tied it so the red thread shows on the front. We made about five ties along each seam line at the corner and center points of each square.

Feather Stitch

Sally Korte and Alice Strebel formed their company, Kindred Spirits, in 1986 when they began publishing patterns and books. Their designs have been featured in many national publications The two lecture and teach nationally and internationally. Their on-line shop is on the web at www.kindredspiritsdesigns.com.

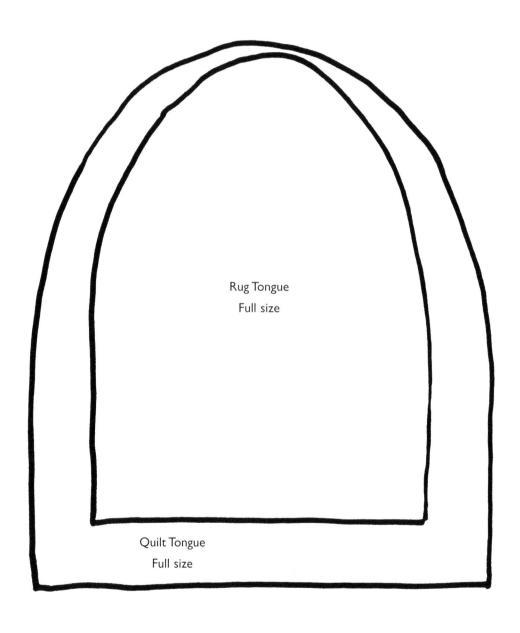

Rug Tongue

Full size

Quilt Tongue

Full size

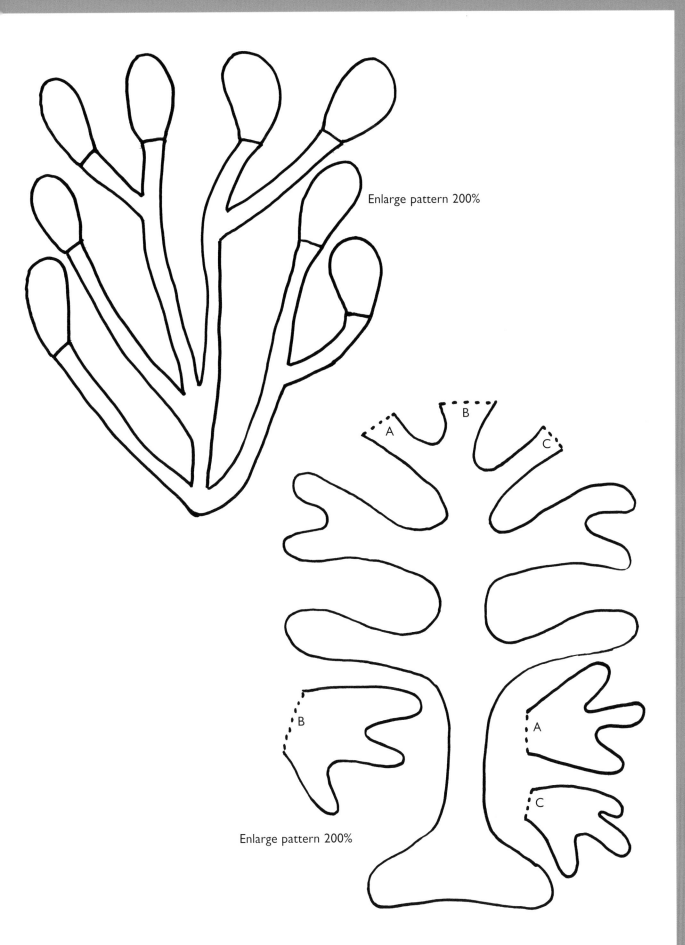

Enlarge pattern 200%

Enlarge pattern 200%

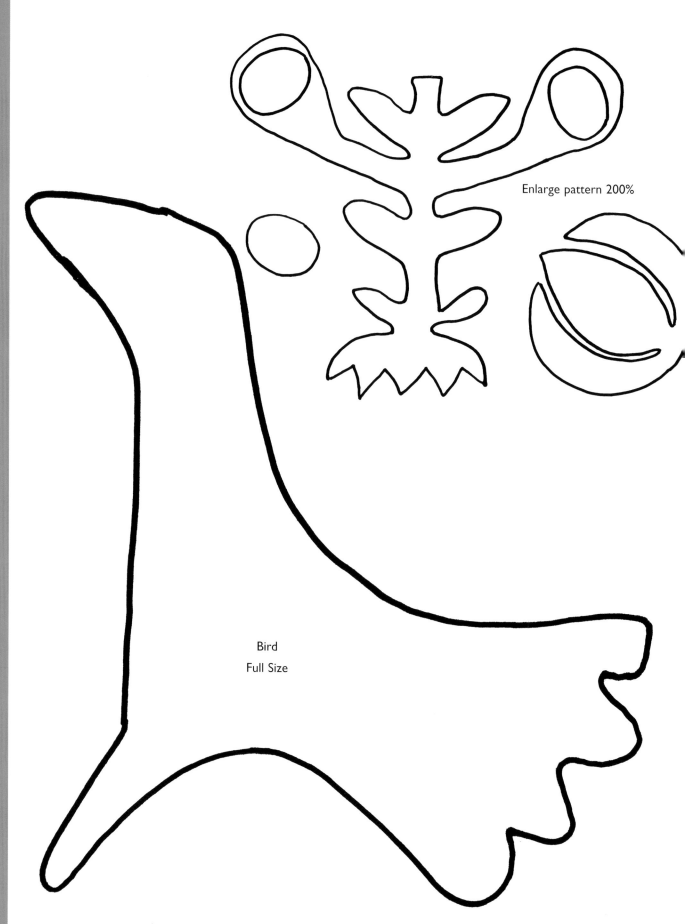

Enlarge pattern 200%

Bird
Full Size

Star
Full Size

Fruit Theorem

Theorem painting is considered traditional folk art and was especially popular in the 19th century in this country. There are many examples of theorem painting in folk art museums across the country. It was popular because the untrained artist could go through several steps and, with the help of stencils, duplicate a painting. Some clever artists would devise their own drawings and then follow the steps to completion. The less talented painter would be given the numbered line drawing and even pre-cut stencils to help achieve the final theorem. Some antique theorems have obviously come out of a classroom setting as more than one rendition of a given work can be seen in museums. Sheri's hooked rug translates the design into wool and reinterprets the colors.

Fruit Theorem Painting

BY NANCY ROSIER

MATERIALS

- Four 13"x 19" clear .005 acetate sheets
- Masking tape
- Black fine point permanent marker suitable for acetate
- Craft knife with several #11 blades
- Glass size 16" x 20" for stencil-cutting surface
- One 11" x 17" sheet of 2-ply white paperboard
- Repositional spray mount artist's adhesive
- Palette pad
- Tweezers for removing excess lint
- Turpentine or oil paint solvent
- Scissors
- Toothpicks for mixing paints
- Stencil brushes, if preferred
- Round pointed oil brush size #0 for detail work
- One yard of 100% cotton twill-back velveteen in white eggshell (AWB Velvets at 1-800-224-7167 has this). You may wish to substitute a fabric from your local fabric store. Try something similar to cotton velvet in texture.
- Oil paints: yellow ochre, burnt umber, cadmium red, Prussian blue, oxide of chromium, raw umber, burnt sienna, Windsor yellow, alizarin crimson, permanent green light, black, and gray
- Sponge, optional
- Brewed coffee, optional
- Towel, optional

DIRECTIONS

1. Enlarge the line drawing to 11" x 17".
2. Cut four acetate sheets 13" x 19".
3. Tape down the line drawing and place the first acetate sheet over the drawing and tape it down.
4. Number the first acetate sheet #1 and trace only the #1 areas of the design. Proceed to sheet #2 and trace only the #2 areas. Continue until all four sheets are traced.
5. Tape the traced acetate sheets to the glass surface and cut stencils with a craft knife.
6. With the nap of the fabric lying toward you (when you run the palm of your hand down the fabric toward yourself, the nap is smoothed down instead of roughed up), cut the fabric 19" wide x 13" high.
7. Spray paperboard with the artist's adhesive and position fabric over the board with the fabric extending over each side and the nap toward you. Fold fabric over the edge of the paperboard and use masking tape to anchor it on the back.
8. Place stencil #1 on top of mounted fabric, making sure the fabric nap is lying toward the bottom of the design, and tape it down.

9. Cut scraps of velveteen approximately 12" x 3" to use for applying the paint and as test strips, or use a stencil brush.

10. Mix any colors necessary on the palette with a toothpick (see Colors—Mixing & Applying). You won't need a lot of paint for each color, perhaps the size of the end of your index finger. You do want enough to cover the areas needed so you don't have to mix more later.

11. Take a strip of fabric and place it over your index finger. Dip it in the desired paint. Rub most of the paint off on a separate piece of fabric until it appears smooth. Use a clean piece of fabric for each application. Work from the outside edges of the stencil hole inward.

12. If you have a separate color coat to apply on this area, do it now. You want to shade and blend colors.

13. Apply the appropriate paint colors to all the open areas in stencil #1, then stencil #2, and proceed through all four stencils. A stencil can immediately be put on the area previously painted. It will not mess up the previous work, but do place the stencil carefully, and do not move it back and forth.

14. After all stencils are finished, use the edge of one of your stencils to form the table line. Simply dab the rest of the table color into the design.

15. Now you are ready to use the detail brush to fill in any gaps in the design and any detail work you couldn't do before, such as leaf veins, bird decorations, cherry stems, butterfly, etc. To make your paint flow easily, first dip your brush in the turpentine and then the paint. Be very careful to always test your paint on scrap material to see that it will not smear.

16. Sign your name and date.

17. Leave the painting mounted for several days until dry.

18. If you want to "age" the dried painting, pull it off the board. Place it on a towel and dab it with a coffee-filled sponge. Allow to dry. Then remount it by spraying adhesive once again on the same board and centering the painting. Fold over the edges and tape down with masking tape. It's ready to slip into a frame.

Nancy Rosier sells her theorem paintings at fine art and craft shows across the country. You may contact her at Rosier Period Art, 1 Somerset Court, Williamsburg, VA 23188. Email rosierart@earthlink.net, web site www.rosier-period-art.com.

Colors—Mixing & Applying

Birds—Begin with a base coat of yellow ochre applied evenly. Next apply burnt umber for shading, working the color from the outer edges inward. Use a small amount of cadmium red on the birds' breasts. Take a curved piece of acetate to guide you as you brush the red and blue lines of the tail and wing of the bird. Paint the decorative lines of the birds freehand at the end.

Birds' beaks and eyes—Burnt umber for both.

Butterfly—Black for the body and the trim of the wings. The base of the wings is Windsor yellow.

Cherries—The same color as the watermelon. The stems are burnt umber and are painted with a detail brush at the end.

Grapes—A mix of Prussian blue with a touch of raw umber to tone down the blue. Shading is especially important, as there is only one color.

Large leaves—These begin with two large stencils, which will first be painted yellow ochre. Later the second step will be another stencil that will be painted oxide of chromium. The last step will be detailing the vines of the leaves, which is done with the detail brush at the end of painting.

Marble base—Gray

Peaches—These have a base coat of yellow ochre with shading of burnt sienna.

Peach leaves—The color is a mixture of equal amounts of permanent green light and yellow ochre. Shade with oxide of chromium mixed with a small amount of raw umber to darken.

Strawberries—The base coat is Windsor yellow. The second coat is cadmium red, leaving some of the yellow to show through. The dots on the strawberries are oxide of chromium, applied with the detail brush at the end.

Strawberry leaves—These are painted with oxide of chromium, being careful to shade.

Watermelon—The main color is alizarin crimson mixed with a touch of burnt umber to tone down the color. Do not fill in the watermelon completely; leave a little white showing as you come up against the rind.

Watermelon rind—The base coat is yellow ochre. Over the ochre put a mixed color of permanent green light and Prussian blue, letting the ochre show through some. Carefully smear the rind color inward.

Enlarge pattern 185%

This is an original design made especially for this book and your personal use only, not for resale.

Fruit Theorem Hooked Rug

ADAPTED FROM A DESIGN BY NANCY ROSIER,

HOOKED BY SHERI BENNETT

MATERIALS

- Backing: 30" x 36" piece of linen, monk's cloth, or rug warp
- 100% wool in #6 (³/₁₆") and #8 (¹/₄") cuts. Remember to keep contrast in mind as you choose your wool colors. You want your fruit and leaf colors to stand out from each other and from the background.

Peaches

- 5" x 12" piece of light peach
- 5" x 5" piece of medium peach
- Scraps of dark peach for the vein in the peach
- Scraps of two shades of green for the leaves
- Scraps of brown for the stems

Strawberries

- Scraps of 3 or 4 shades of red for the berries
- Scrap of yellow for the seeds
- Scraps of one green for the leaves and tendrils (different from the watermelon rind, as they overlap)

Cherries

- 2" x 6" piece of red for the cherries
- Brown scraps for the stems

Grapes

- Scraps of four or more shades of purple

Grape Leaves

- Scraps of medium or dark green for the outline of the leaves and tendrils
- 9" x 10" lavender and green spot dye for the leaves
- Scraps of dark purple for the veins

Bluebirds

- 4" x 8" piece of dark blue
- 4" x 6" piece of medium blue
- 8" x 9" piece of light blue
- Scraps of rusty red will do for the breasts of the birds
- Scrap of orange for the beaks
- Scrap of brown or dark blue for the eyes

Watermelon

- 3" x 10" piece of cream wool
- 3" x 10" piece of pale pink
- 3" x 10" piece of pink
- 3" x 10" piece of medium pink
- 4" x 10" piece of dark pink or light red
- 1" x 8" piece of red
- Scraps of medium and dark green for the rind (different from strawberry leaves)
- Scraps of dark brownish green or brown for the seeds

Butterfly

- Scraps of three shades of mauve or purple for the wings: light, medium, and dark
- Scraps of brown for the body and spots on the wings

Background

- 14" x 25" piece of medium light green for the table
- 18" x 48" piece of pale green mottled wool for the wall

Borders

- 18" x 35" piece of medium dark green
- 12" x 20" piece of dark green

Strawberries

Watermelon

Background

Grapes

DIRECTIONS

1. Enlarge and transfer the pattern to the backing. I used linen, but monk's cloth or rug warp are perfectly acceptable. These motifs were hooked in a #6 cut.

2. Hook the fruit in front of the watermelon first. Start with the peaches. On both peaches, hook the right sides with a light peach spot-dyed wool. Hook them in a circular direction. The left sides of each peach were hooked with a medium shade of peach wool in a half-round direction. Be sure there is enough contrast between these two shades. In the crease between the two sides, hook a very narrow strip of dark peach. Cut a #6-cut strip in half lengthwise for this strip. Also, use a very narrow strip of brown for the stems. Hook the leaves in two shades of green. Hook each leaf with the lighter shade of green on the left side and a darker shade on the right side.

3. Next, hook the strawberries. Use different shades of red scraps. On the two strawberries that overlap, hook the left side of the top berry with a lighter red and the right side of the bottom berry in a darker red to separate them visually. Use lighter shades on the tops of the berries and darker shades on the bottom. Hook the leaves and tendrils using a medium shade of green wool that is different from your watermelon rind greens. Add the seeds after you have hooked the berries—cut a very narrow strip of yellow and hook it in between the red loops in five or six places. One loop is enough.

4. The grapes and leaves should be next. Outline each grape and fill. Hook each grape in a different shade. You may use the same color more than once, but no two grapes of the same color should touch. Contrast between each grape is important, or they will blend together. Outline the leaves next, and then hook the tendrils with the green you have chosen. Hook the veins of the leaves with the dark purple scraps and then fill in the leaves with the lavender and green spot dye.

5. Now we come to the watermelon. The rind is hooked in three rows. Starting with the darkest green, hook the first line of the rind. Then hook a line of medium green on top of the first line. One line of cream follows that. After you finish the rind, hook the seeds with the brownish green or brown. The next rows will be hooked perpendicularly to your rind lines. Hook the next four colors in bands approximately $1/2$" wide. Starting with the cream wool, hook perpendicular lines unevenly around the rind. Some lines will be taller than others. Skip a space every now and then. These will be filled in by the next color. Called "fingering," this technique helps to blend the different rows of colors together without a definite line. Follow the cream rows with the pale pink wool. Fill in any

Cherries

Blue birds

Peaches

Grape leaves

spaces that you left in the previous row. Again, hook uneven lines, some shorter and some longer. Follow this color with rows of the pink, medium pink, dark pink, or light red, and end with the red. Use more dark pink than the other colors and a little red in the very middle of the top of the slice of melon. As you come to seeds, just end and clip and start again on the other side. Remember to hook perpendicularly from the rind. Your hooking lines will angle in toward the center.

6. The cherries and stems are hooked in red and brown scraps. Outline and fill each cherry. Hook the stems and the twig in the other bird's mouth with your brown scraps. The birds come next. Hook the beaks with the orange scraps and hook the eyes with a scrap of dark blue or brown. Also, hook the lines on the tails with the dark blue. Now, outline and hook the heads and bodies of both birds with the light blue wool, excluding the wings. Outline the wings with the medium blue and hook the sections of the wings closest to the shoulders with the dark blue. Then hook the rest of the *back* wing with the light blue and the rest of the *front* wing with the medium blue. Remember that contrast is important to keep the wings from disappearing into each other.

7. Last, but not least, is the butterfly. Outline the wings with the dark purple. Hook the body and the dots on the wings with brown scraps. You may want to use a very narrow brown strip for the antennae and spots on the wings. Fill in the top, larger sections of the wings with the light purple. The back, smaller sections of the wings are hooked with the medium purple wool.

8. Now comes the background. Use #8 cut wool to finish your rug. Remember to hook this cut the same height as you hooked the #6 cut. Hook one row of your darkest green border wool on the inner borderline surrounding the center area. Hook the table next with the medium light green in straight rows, horizontally, across the piece. End, clip, and start again as you come to the fruit and leaves. To keep the lines straight, follow a thread of your backing across your piece as you hook. The wall behind the fruit is hooked with the palest green. Outline the birds, butterfly, fruit, and leaves that extend above the table with the background color. Then the wall can be hooked in wavy lines, curved sections, or vertical strips, as you choose. I chose to hook small curved sections throughout.

9. For the border, hook seven rows of medium dark green outside the dark green inner borderline. End with two rows of dark green around the outer edge. If you choose to sign your rug, you may put this in the border in a lighter contrasting green. Dating your rug is also a good idea.

Line drawing of Fruit Theorem rug. The pattern should be enlarged to 14¹/₂" x 20¹/₂" for use. Add a 2" border around the pattern.

10. Finish the rug in your favorite manner. I finished the edges of the rug with the same dark green wool that I used in the border. I covered narrow cotton cording with the dark green wool and stitched it to the rug, by hand, as close as possible to the last row of hooking. I then bound the rug in the usual manner with rug binding tape on the back. You might also like to make a label for the back of your rug. Including information such as where you hooked it, when you hooked it, and if it was a gift, will be helpful to future generations who will admire your work and treasure it!

Sheri Bennett is an avid and accomplished student of rug hooking. Her work was selected for A Celebration of Hand-Hooked Rugs XI *and* XIV, *published by* Rug Hooking *magazine. She lives in Kentucky.*

Pumpkins in the Round

Vintage Halloween collectibles were the inspiration for this hooked rug. The pumpkin faces are reminiscent of paper lanterns, and the circles mimic the hypnotic eyes of devils and goblins. Using a variety of 100-percent wool textures and scraps in a classic black and orange Halloween color scheme lends a time-worn look to the tablemat. It is finished with a single crochet using black and orange eyelash yarn. What a great rug to make for your spooky Halloween table.

The penny rug mat uses the same pumpkin faces as the hooked rug. Use 100-percent wool textures in neutrals, oranges, and antique blacks. It calls for basic sewing stitches including the blanket and the straight stitch.

Pumpkins in the Round Hooked Rug

By Jenny Rupp and Lisa Yeago

To complete the hooked rug project, you will need to know basic rug hooking (see page 103) and crocheting techniques. It helps to have a sewing machine, although all the sewing required can be done by hand.

MATERIALS

- 29" x 29" piece of rug backing (monk's cloth or linen)
- Eight $1/4$-yard pieces of different orange textured wool
- $1/2$ yard of assorted medium value neutrals: oatmeal, beige, taupe, etc.
- $1/2$ yard of assorted antique black
- $1/8$ yard of dull gold
- basic hooking supplies
- needle and thread
- 1 skein SR Kertzer Ltd (Italian) MultiFizz eyelash yarn—black and orange shade 911, lot 8621, 1.75 ounces
- #5 crochet hook

DIRECTIONS

1. Enlarge the pattern (page 83) and trace it onto the center of the backing. If the backing is light, you can place it on a light table or against a sunny window to trace the pattern. If you have dark backing, you can transfer the pattern by using red dot tracing material or vinyl screening. Both these products are available at large discount stores. Lay the screening on top of the pattern and trace it. Then lay the screening on top of the rug backing and trace it with a black permanent marker. The screen pattern should be stored rolled up and can be used many times.

2. For this circular pattern, it is important to prepare the backing properly for eventual finishing. Once the pattern is traced onto the backing, sew a straight stitch along the design line border. This will keep the backing from fraying when you cut off the excess and clip the curves. Next, measure out $1^{1}/2$" from the design edge and sew a straight stitch line. If you do not have a sewing machine, you can do this by hand, but remember to backstitch every other stitch. Now you are ready to hook.

3. Wool can be purchased or dyed for this project. To create a vintage look, incorporate textured wools such as herringbones, tweeds, and plaids into the piece. All the orange, neutral/putty, and gold wool in this project are of medium value. The antique black provides the contrast. If you are dyeing wool, use many different smaller pieces of wool when you over-dye to get a variety of textures and values. We have provided dye formulas if you want to dye your wool.

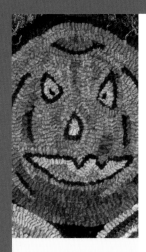

Dyeing

All the dye formulas use ProChem dyes in 1 cup boiling water over $^1/_2$ yard wool. Adjust the amounts of wool and dye for greater or smaller quantities.

Orange

$^1/_2$ tsp Spiced Pumpkin #230

over oatmeal, gray, tan, brown textures

Antique Black

$^1/_4$ + $^1/_8$ tsp Black #672

$^1/_8$ + $^1/_{16}$ tsp Brown #503

over dark gray, brown, green, purple, red textures

Neutral/Putty

$^1/_{32}$ tsp Chestnut #560

$^1/_{128}$ tsp Yellow #119

$^1/_{128}$ tsp Brown #503

over taupe, beige, oatmeal, tan textures

Dull Gold

$^1/_4$ tsp Mustard #122

over gray textures

See page 55 for suggested dyeing procedures.

4. The majority of wool used in this project is #8 cut ($^1/_4$"). A narrower #6 cut ($^3/_{16}$") is used for outlining the eyes, nose, mouth, and accent lines on the pumpkins. If you don't have a #6 cutter head, just cut #8 strips and trim them thinner with a sharp pair of scissors. It is critical that you hook well inside the lines. Hooking tends to expand the shape as you hook. When hooking circles, staying inside the lines means the circles will retain their round shape and not become lumpy and misshapen as they meet each other. Keep this in mind constantly when hooking adjoining circles.

5. For the pumpkins, cut some antique black in a #6 cut and hook the outlines of the eyes, nose, mouth, and accent lines. Fill in with dull gold. Each pumpkin is hooked with two different orange colors. One should be a bit lighter and the other darker. These pumpkins are "shaded." That means that the top of the pumpkin is lighter than the bottom. By mid pumpkin, you should be introducing some dark

orange into the lighter orange. Each dark accent line is hooked with a dark orange beside it. This simple shading creates some interest and movement in the shape. Hook each pumpkin before moving on to the rings.

6. The circle rings consist of a three-layer pattern: cream, black, and then orange. Here again, remember to start that first outside row inside the line. Work from the outside to the center. You will hook 14 rows before ending with a solid black center. A tip to remember when hooking rings: each ring must be the same strip width. If you start with a #8 cut, complete that ring with a #8. You can do each ring in a different width, but each ring must be completed with the same strip width. Don't hook too tightly or the circle will rise in the center.

7. The center circle is a different pattern that provides some rest for the eye. Hook nine rows of various neutrals, five rows of orange, and complete the center with black.

8. The space between the circles is filled in with antique black. Follow the perimeter of the circles with two rows of antique black.

9. Stand back and look at the hooked piece with a critical eye for color. Sometimes standing back and squinting helps point out areas that are too prominent or that fade away. You especially don't want one or two rings to really stand out. Check the back for loose loops and hanging ends.

10. Steaming a hooked piece is important, especially for a round rug. Round rugs tend to rise up in the center, and steaming helps settle the rug back down and will smooth out the lumpy spots. Take an old white dishtowel and get it wet. Wring some of the water out and lay the towel over the center of your rug. Place a hot iron on the wet towel. You will hear the sizzle. Don't press on the iron, but move it out towards the border of the rug. When you have reached the limits of the wet towel, rewet it and continue to the edges. While the rug is damp, you can pull gently on the edges to get it into shape. Turn the rug to the back and steam again. Allow to dry completely.

11. To prepare for finishing the edges, trim off the excess backing to the outer line of sewing. You will have to clip the curves. Don't clip all the way to the hooking yet.

12. Get a needle and thread ready to baste the edge. Fold the backing in half towards the last row of hooking. Fold it forward again to create a little lip right up against the hooking. Pin and baste it down. Work your way around the perimeter of the rug. As you get into the curves, you may need to clip the dips deeper. You want to create a smooth, even edge that will be the foundation for a row of single crochet (or whipping).

13. It may be necessary at this point to steam only the edges that you have just basted in order to make them lie flat. Allow to dry.

14. After you have basted around the piece, begin crocheting (or whipping). My favorite crocheting yarn is worsted weight 100% wool yarn. I use a size 00 steel crochet hook. Begin crocheting with the rug in your lap, right side up, with the edge away from you. Insert the hook next to your last row of hooking and pull a loop through. Take two chain stitches and then single crochet down the row. Pay attention to the spacing of your stitches. Depending on the thickness of the yarn and the weave of your backing fabric, you will have to adjust how many holes to skip in between each single crochet. Occasionally lay the rug down on a flat surface to check for buckling. You want your finished piece to lie flat.

15. To turn a corner, take two single crochets in the hole right before the corner, then take a chain stitch. Then take two single crochets in the hole right after the corner and continue as before down the new side.

16. To end, cut the yarn off and pull through the last loop. Weave under the tail from the beginning and the end.

Pumpkins in the Round Penny Rug

By Jenny Rupp and Lisa Yeago

MATERIALS

- $3/8$ yard of assorted antique black textures
- $1/8$ yard of assorted orange textures
- $1/8$ yard of assorted neutrals
- Large embroidery needle
- Assorted threads for appliqué in orange, black, and tan (we like to use Aurifil Lana Wool Thread, but two strands of embroidery floss would be a good substitute)

DIRECTIONS

1. Enlarge the patterns as specified. Copy each individual pattern piece onto white paper and cut it out.

2. Cut out 14 of the largest circles, using a variety of black textured wool (a full-size penny pattern appears on page 84). Cut out the remaining circles using the picture as a guide for colors. The pumpkin faces are cut out of oranges with the facial features cut out of black and neutrals. Again refer to the color photo for color suggestions. In the stitching instructions below, the colors used will be shown in parentheses.

3. To put the pennies together, stack the center circle as shown in the photo. Begin by stitching the smallest circle (we used black) to the next larger circle (orange). Use a blanket stitch in a contrasting color. A diagram of the blanket stitch is shown on the next page.

4. Stitch the orange circle to the next larger one (neutral). Again choose a contrasting thread and use the blanket stitch. The final step is to attach the penny stack to the large black circle. Page 85 shows a diagram of the color placement for the center circle.

5. The remaining penny circles are constructed the same way with a different color arrangement. The diagram on page 85 shows the placement of the colors.

Remember to build the penny from the small circle out.

6. Make three of the outside penny circles.

7. Cut out the pumpkin face features, using black for the outline color and oranges or neutrals for the inside of each feature. Begin by stitching the black facial features to the orange circle. Using the blanket stitch here is difficult because the pieces are so small. We use a small straight stitch instead. It is much easier and looks great for this purpose.

8. Next stitch the smaller facial features on top of the black pieces. The last step is to blanket stitch the orange circle to a large black circle. The diagram on page 85 shows the placement of colors for the pumpkin face circles.

9. Attach a large black circle to the back of each completed penny. Again use the blanket stitch and orange thread.

10. The final step is to join the pennies together. Arrange the pennies right side up. Flip one penny onto a neighbor, right sides together. Join them together using black thread and a tiny whip stitch. Tie off the thread and lay the pennies down right side up. Repeat this process until all of the pennies are attached.

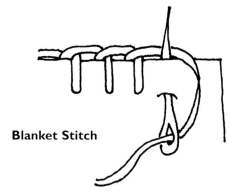

Blanket Stitch

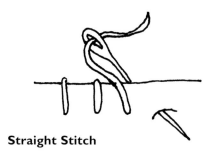

Straight Stitch

Jenny Rupp and Lisa Yeago have more than 20 years combined experience making hooked rugs. They design patterns, teach classes, and dye wool and yarn for rug hookers. Their articles have appeared in Rug Hooking *magazine, and they are working on their first book. They own the Potted Pear, a rug hooking business, at 7045 Pinemill Drive, West Chester, OH 45069. Web site www.pottedpear.com, telephone (513) 759-5301.*

Finished size is 25" x 25" for the hooked rug and 13" x 13" for the penny rug.

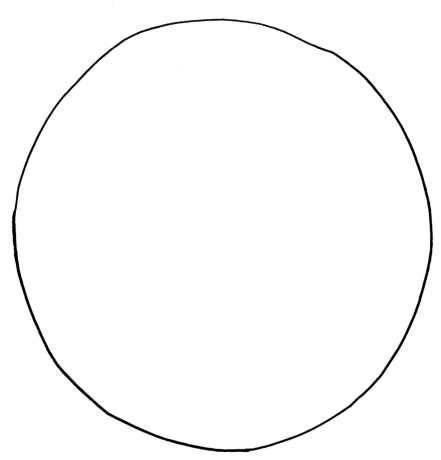

Full size Penny for Penny Rug

Make 14 (Black)

Center Penny Circle

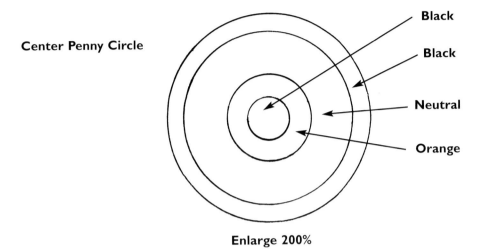

Black

Black

Neutral

Orange

Enlarge 200%

Outside Penny Circles

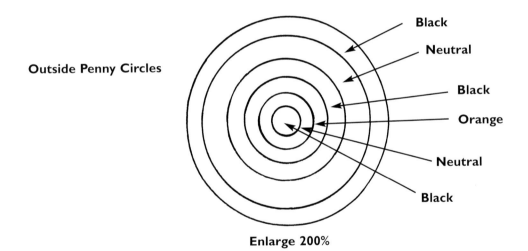

Black

Neutral

Black

Orange

Neutral

Black

Enlarge 200%

Pumpkin Face drawing

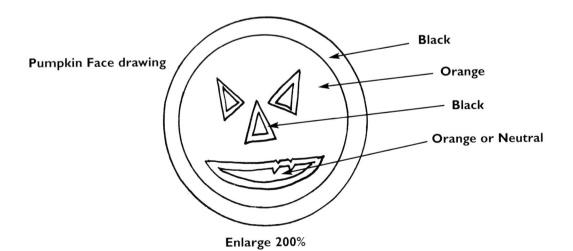

Black

Orange

Black

Orange or Neutral

Enlarge 200%

Christmas Star

Decorate any room for the holidays in no time at all with a festive ensemble which includes a lap quilt, pillows, table runner, ornaments, and counted cross stitch piece. One simple block design was used for each project. Make one or all—but the more the merrier!

Christmas Star Lap Quilt

By Mark Lipinski

INTERMEDIATE
Finished block size:
8" x 8" (sewn into quilt)
Number of blocks:
16 pieced, 9 setting
Finished quilt size:
58" x 58"

MATERIALS

Yardage is based on 42"-wide fabric.

- 1$^{1}/_{4}$ yards of green tonal fabric (includes binding)
- 1$^{1}/_{2}$ yards of cream dot fabric
- 2$^{1}/_{3}$ yards of red tonal fabric
- 64" x 64" piece of backing fabric
- 64"x 64" piece of batting
- Thread in colors to match fabrics
- Rotary cutter, ruler, and mat
- Basic sewing supplies

CUTTING

From the green tonal fabric, cut:

- Five 2$^{7}/_{8}$" x 42" strips; re-cut into sixty-four 2$^{7}/_{8}$" squares
- Six 2$^{1}/_{2}$" x 42" strips (for binding)
- Five 1$^{1}/_{2}$" x 42" strips (for inner border)

From the cream dot fabric, cut:

- One to two 8$^{1}/_{2}$" x 42" strips; re-cut into five 8$^{1}/_{2}$" squares (for setting squares)
- Ten 2$^{7}/_{8}$" x 42" strips; re-cut into one hundred twenty-eight 2$^{7}/_{8}$" squares

From the red tonal fabric, cut:

- One 12$^{5}/_{8}$" x 42" strip; re-cut into three 12$^{5}/_{8}$" squares, then cut each square diagonally in half twice (for setting triangles)
- One 8$^{1}/_{2}$" x 42" strip; re-cut into four 8$^{1}/_{2}$" squares (for setting squares)
- One 6$^{5}/_{8}$" x 42" strip; re-cut into two 6$^{5}/_{8}$" squares; then cut diagonally in half once (for corner triangles)
- Six 5$^{1}/_{2}$" x 42" strips (for outer borders)
- Five 2$^{7}/_{8}$" x 42" strips; re-cut into sixty-four 2$^{7}/_{8}$" squares

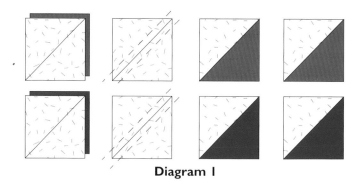

Diagram 1

Block Diagrams

DIRECTIONS

Use a ¹/₄" seam allowance throughout. Sew all pieces with right sides together and raw edges even, using matching thread unless otherwise indicated. Press seam allowance toward the darker fabrics.

1. Draw a diagonal line on the wrong side of the cream dot squares. Place each square, right sides together, with a red square or a green square. Following **Diagram 1**, stitch ¹/₄" away from each side of the marked lines, then cut apart along the lines to yield a total of 128 red/cream units and 128 green/cream units.

2. Referring to the **Block Diagrams** and noting orientation, sew the units assembled in Step 1 together to make eight red/cream blocks and eight green/cream

blocks. Trim blocks evenly to measure 8¹/₂" x 8¹/₂".

3. Referring to the **Quilt Layout Diagram**, sew the red/cream blocks and green/cream blocks together with the setting squares in diagonal rows. Stitch the setting triangles to the ends of the rows; then piece the rows together. Add the corner triangles. Trim the quilt top evenly, leaving ¹/₄" past the block corners.

4. *Inner border.* Sew the 1¹/₂" x 42" green tonal strips, short ends together, into one long strip. Measure the quilt top vertically through the center and cut two lengths to this measurement. Sew to opposite sides of the quilt top. Next, measure the quilt top horizontally through the center, including the side border strips. Stitch to the remaining sides of

Quilt Layout Diagram

the quilt top. Press seams toward the borders.

5. **Outer border.** Sew the 5¹/₂" x 42" red strips, short ends together, into one long strip and attach to the outer border in the same manner as the inner border.

6. Place the quilt top, right side up, on top of the batting. Place the backing, wrong side up, on top of the quilt top. Baste the layers together and quilt as desired. Trim backing and batting even with raw edge of quilt top.

7. Sew the 2¹/₂" green tonal strips, short ends together, into one long strip. Fold in half lengthwise, wrong sides together, and press fold. Leaving an 8" tail, align raw edges, and sew to the quilt top through all layers, mitering the corners and overlapping the ends. Turn binding strip to back of quilt and blind stitch in place.

INTERMEDIATE
Finished block size:
8" x 8"
Finished runner size:
15" x 50"

Christmas Star Table Runner

BY MARK LIPINSKI

MATERIALS

Yardage is based on 42"-wide useable fabric.

- $1/2$ yard of green tonal
- $3/4$ yard of red tonal (includes binding)
- $3/4$ yard of cream dot
- 19" x 54" piece of backing fabric
- 19" x 54" piece of batting
- Thread in colors to match fabrics
- Rotary cutter, ruler, and mat
- Basic sewing supplies

CUTTING

From the green tonal fabric, cut:

- Two $2^7/8$" x 42" strips; re-cut into sixteen $2^7/8$" squares, then cut diagonally in half
- Six 1" x 42" strips (for first and third borders)

From the red tonal fabric, cut:

- Two $2^7/8$" x 42" strips; re-cut into twenty-four $2^7/8$" squares, then cut diagonally in half
- Three $1^1/2$" x 42" strips (for second border)
- Four $2^1/2$" x 42" strips (for binding)

From the cream dot fabric, cut:

- Three $2^7/8$" x 42" strips; re-cut into forty $2^7/8$" squares, then cut diagonally in half
- One $12^5/8$" square; cut diagonally in half twice to make four setting triangles
- Two $6^5/8$" squares; cut diagonally in half once to make four corner triangles

Diagram 1

Diagram 2

DIRECTIONS

1. Following **Diagrams 1** and **2**, sew a
   cream triangle to each of the red and
   green triangles to make 44 red/cream
   units and 32 green/cream units.

2. Referring to the **Block Diagrams**, use
   the units assembled in Step 1 to assemble
   two red/cream blocks and two green/
   cream blocks. Use the remaining units to
   assemble two partial red/cream blocks as
   shown in the **Partial Block Diagram**.

3. Following the **Runner Layout Diagram**
   on page 94, lay out the pieced blocks on
   point, together with the cream quarter-
   square setting triangles and half-square
   corner triangles. Sew the pieces together
   on the diagonal as shown. Trim evenly.

4. Sew three of the green strips, short ends
   together, into one long strip. Measure the
   runner top lengthwise through the center.
   Cut two lengths to this measurement and
   stitch to the long sides of the runner top.
   Next, measure widthwise through the
   center, including the side border strips.
   Cut two more lengths to this measurement and sew to the short sides of the
   runner top.

5. Using the 1½" x 42" red strips and the
   remaining green strips, attach the second
   and third borders in the same manner.

Block Diagrams

Partial Block Diagram

6. Layer the runner, right side up, on top of the batting and the wrong side of the backing fabric. Baste the layers together and quilt in the ditch, in an overall meandering design, or as desired.

7. Sew the $2^{1}/_{2}$" x 42" red strips, short ends together, into one long strip. Fold in half lengthwise with wrong sides facing. Leaving an 8" tail, align the raw edges of the strip with the raw edges of the runner top and stitch to the runner through all layers, mitering the corners and overlapping the ends. Trim excess. Turn binding to back of quilt and blind stitch in place.

Runner Layout Diagram

Christmas Star Pillow Pair

By Mark Lipinski

MATERIALS

For two pillows:

- $3/4$ yard of cream dot fabric
- 1 yard of green tonal fabric
- 1 yard of red tonal fabric
- 1 yard of muslin
- Thread in colors to match fabrics
- Two 15" squares of batting
- 12" pillow form
- Rotary cutter, ruler, and mat
- Basic sewing supplies

CUTTING

From the cream dot fabric, cut:

- Four $2^3/8$" x 42" strips; recut into sixty-four $2^3/8$" squares
- Two $13^1/2$" x $13^1/2$" squares of backing fabric

From each of the red and green tonal fabrics, cut:

- Two $2^3/8$" x 42" strips; re-cut into thirty-two $2^3/8$" squares (for blocks)
- One $1^1/2$" x 42" strip; recut into four $1^1/2$" x $6^1/2$" strips and one $1^1/2$" square (for sashing)
- Two 5" x 42" strips (for ruffle)

BEGINNER

Finished block size:

6" x 6"

Finished pillow size:

13" x 13"

(without ruffle)

DIRECTIONS

Use a $^1/_4$" seam allowance throughout. Sew all pieces with right sides together and raw edges even using matching thread unless otherwise indicated. Press seam allowance toward the darker fabrics.

1. Draw a diagonal line on the wrong side of the cream dot squares. Place each square, right sides together, with a red square or a green square. Following **Diagram 1**, stitch $^1/_4$" away from each side of the marked lines, then cut apart along the lines to yield a total of 32 red/cream units and 32 green/cream units.

2. Referring to the **Block Diagrams** and noting orientation, sew the units assembled in Step 1 together to make four red/cream blocks and four green/cream blocks. Trim blocks evenly to measure $6^1/_2$" x $6^1/_2$".

3. Referring to the **Pillow Layout Diagrams**, sew the red/cream blocks together with the $1^1/_2$" x $6^1/_2$" green sashing strips and $1^1/_2$" red square. Sew the green/cream blocks together with the $1^1/_2$" x $6^1/_2$" red sashing strips and $1^1/_2$" green square. Trim the pillow tops evenly to measure $13^1/_2$" x $13^1/_2$".

4. Cut a 15" square for each pillow from the muslin. Layer each pillow top right side up on top of a piece of batting and the muslin backing. Baste the layers together and quilt in the ditch along the seam lines.

5. Sew the two red ruffle strips, short ends together, to make one long strip. Sew the short ends of the strip together to form a loop. With wrong sides facing, fold the loop in half widthwise and press. Sew a line of basting stitches $^1/_4$" away from the raw edge and pull to gather the ruffle. With fold facing in, align the raw edges of the ruffle with the raw edge of the

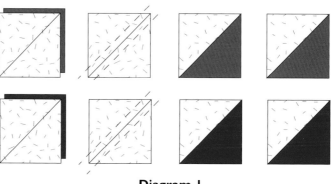

Diagram 1

Block Diagrams   **Pillow Layout Diagrams**

green/cream block pillow top and pin all the way around. Topstitch. Repeat with the green ruffle strips and red/cream block pillow top.

6. Making sure that the ruffle is positioned correctly, pin each quilted pillow top, right

sides together, with a 13^1/$_2$" square of cream dot backing fabric. Stitch along three sides, leaving an opening on one side for turning. Turn right side out and insert the pillow form. Hand stitch the opening closed.

Christmas Star Ornaments

BY MARK LIPINSKI

MATERIALS

For two ornaments:

- $1/8$ yard of cream dot fabric
- $1/4$ yard of green tonal fabric
- $1/4$ yard of red tonal fabric
- Thread in colors to match fabrics
- Two 6" squares of batting
- Pliers and two 10" lengths of thin- to medium-gauge craft wire
- Four $1/2$"-diameter gold jingle bells
- Basic sewing supplies

CUTTING

From the cream dot fabric, cut:

- One $1^7/8$" x 42" strip; re-cut into sixteen $1^7/8$" squares

From each of the green and red fabrics, cut:

- One 6" square (for backing)
- One $1^7/8$" x 20" strip; re-cut into eight $1^7/8$" squares

DIRECTIONS

Use a $1/4$" seam allowance throughout. Sew all pieces with right sides together and raw edges even using matching thread. Press seams toward the darker fabrics.

1. Draw a diagonal line on the wrong side of the cream dot squares. Place each square right sides together with a red square or a green square. Following **Diagram 1** (page 96), stitch $1/4$" away from each side of the marked lines, then cut apart along the lines to yield a total of 16 red/cream units and 16 green/cream units.

2. Referring to the **Block Diagrams** (page 97) and noting orientation, sew the units assembled in Step 1 together to make one red/cream block and one green/cream block. Trim blocks evenly to measure $4^1/2$" x $4^1/2$".

3. Layer the red/cream block right side up on top of the batting and the wrong side of the 6" square of red backing fabric. Baste the layers together as desired. Quilt in the ditch along all seam lines. Trim batting and backing even with top of block. Layer the green/cream block in the same manner using the 6" square of green backing fabric.

4. Fold each of the $2^1/2$" x 42" red and green strips in half with wrong sides together. Aligning raw edges, sew the red strip to the top of the green/cream block through all layers, mitering the corners and over-lapping the ends. Trim excess. Turn the binding to the back of the block and blind stitch in place. Sew the green strip to the red/cream block in the same manner.

5. Place the ornaments on point and, working from back to front, poke the wire through the binding at the seam line where indicated on the photos. Thread a bell on the end of each wire and use the pliers to curl the ends.

Christmas Star Cross Stitch

By Mark Lipinski

MATERIALS

- DMC 14" x 18" 28-count linen in color 712
- 1 skein of red floss (the featured project used Weeks Dye Works hand-dyed Turkish Red floss No. 2266*)
- 1 skein of green floss (the featured project used Weeks Dye Works hand-dyed Cypress No. 2153*)
- No. 26 tapestry needle

*Visit www.weeksdyeworks.com or call (919) 722-9166 for a retailer near you.

DIRECTIONS

1. To locate the center point of the linen, fold the fabric in half, then in half again. Finger press to crease.

2. Determine the center point of the pattern (see triangle marks located on the pattern grid). Thread the needle with the appropriate color floss and begin stitching the design, working from the center outward across two threads of fabric. **Note:** *If using the hand-dyed floss, do not separate the strands. If using regular six-strand commercial floss, separate two to three strands to work the design.*

3. Finish each color section of the design by running the floss under four or five stitches on the back of the stitchery. (Do not knot the floss.)

Mark Lipinski is a professional quilt designer from Long Valley, New Jersey. He is the vice president of the State Quilt Guild of New Jersey and the Common Threads Quilters. His work has been widely published in a variety of quilting magazines, including The Quilter *and* Fabric Trends. *He also raises honey bees and hens, when he's not working in his design studio. To learn more about Mark, visit his web site at www.pickleroad.com.*

PATTERN GRID FOR CHRISTMAS STAR CROSS STITCH

General Rug Hooking Directions

Basic instructions to help you transfer a pattern, finish a rug, and hook with strips of wool

TRANSFERING A PATTERN TO BACKING

Beginning rug hookers often have problems figuring out how to transfer a printed pattern onto a rug backing (burlap, monk's cloth, etc.). There are several ways to go about it, but the first step in all cases is to decide how big you want your rug to be.

Once you've determined that, a pen, a ruler, and a little arithmetic are needed for one transferring method. Draw a grid over the printed pattern. For a simple pattern, the grid's squares can be large; for a complex one, make them small. Use the same number of squares to draw a grid on the rug backing. To achieve proper proportions, calculate the size of the squares. Say you want your rug to be a 40" square, and you've used 8 squares across the top of your printed pattern's grid. 40÷8=5, so that means your 8 squares on the backing should be 5" on each side. You also used 8 squares down the side of the pattern, so you'll also use eight, 5" squares along the side as well. This grid will allow you to draw fragments of the pattern in the correct spot and in the correct proportion.

Another method employs a copy machine and nylon veiling (available at fabric stores). After you've used the copier to enlarge the pattern to the desired size, tape the veiling over it and trace all the lines onto the veiling. (It helps to have a transparent ruler to get the lines perfectly straight.) Then tape the marked veiling onto the backing. Retrace the lines on the veiling with a felt-tip pen so they bleed through onto the backing.

An iron-on pattern pencil that makes an indelible blue line can also help you transfer. Tape tracing paper over the pattern. Using a light table or a sunny window, trace the design onto the tracing paper with an ordinary pencil; turn the tracing paper over and draw over the lines with the pattern pencil, making a mirror image of the design.

Set your iron on high (cotton setting) and allow it to heat up well. Place the tracing paper with the mirror image down on the backing. Holding the paper securely, iron slowly over the design. Press hard, and do not move the iron around the design. Lift and reposition carefully until you have pressed the entire design. Be patient to allow enough time for the lines to be transferred onto the backing. (The pencil lines turn blue as they transfer.)

To check if the pattern has transferred successfully, lift a corner of the paper carefully so that it doesn't move. When all the lines are clearly visible on the backing, it is ready.

FINISH BEFORE YOU START

Finishing the edges of hooked pieces is critically important to improve their durability, particularly for floor rugs. When walked on for a number of years, poorly finished edges crack and split, requiring reconstruction that may be unsightly.

Unfortunately, even some experienced rug hookers do not finish their edges well. A quick review of common finishing techniques will benefit even the most seasoned rug hookers and may keep beginners from forming bad habits.

Before you begin hooking a pattern, machine stitch two rows around the perimeter as a defense against fraying. Stitch the first row $1/4$" beyond what will be the hooked portion, and the second row $1/4$" beyond the first row ($1/2$" beyond the hooked portion). Overstitch each row of straight stitches with a row of zigzag stitches as shown in Figure 1.

After hooking the entire rug, vacuum it lightly and check it for mistakes. Lay it on a sheet wrong-side up and cover it with a damp towel. Stamp press it lightly with a dry iron to flatten it; do not rub it as if ironing clothing. Rehook bulging or uneven areas before finishing the edges.

The finished edge should be as high as the hooking, so select cording accordingly. Use preshrunk, natural-fiber cording: clothesline, heavy twine, etc.

Fold the backing toward the back side of the rug, about $1/2$" from the hooked

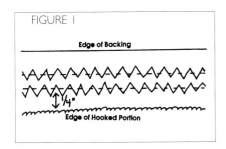

FIGURE 1

Edge of Backing

$1/4$"

Edge of Hooked Portion

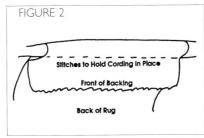

FIGURE 2

Stitches to Hold Cording in Place

Front of Backing

Back of Rug

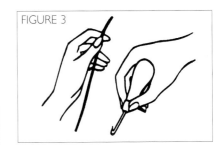

FIGURE 3

portion. Insert the cording and baste it into place with thread as shown in Figure 2. When whipped with yarn, the cording preserves the edge of the rug by taking the pressure of footsteps.

Dye woolen yarn to match your border or to coordinate with your color plan. After the cording is in place, whip the yarn around it with a blunt needle. You will use about one foot of yarn for each inch of whipping.

To whip the edge, simply sew yarn around the cording that is already covered with backing. Whip right up to the edge of the hooked portion on the front, out the back of the rug, around the cording, and down into the front again.

Continue around the perimeter of the rug, making sure the whipping covers the backing evenly. Do not start at a corner. At the corners, you will need to whip more stitches to cover the backing, and you will not be able to create perfectly square corners.

On the back side of the rug, hand-stitch 1 1/4" cotton binding tape right up to the edge of the whipping. Miter the tape and the backing at the corners. Cut away the excess backing so the raw edge is hidden under the tape. Finally, sew the inner edge of the tape between loops in the back of the hooked portion to cover the raw edge of the backing.

Sew a label onto the back of your rug. Include your name and location, the name and dimensions of the rug, the designer, the date, and any other pertinent information. Give the rug one final steam press as described above, using a much wetter towel. Lay it flat to dry.

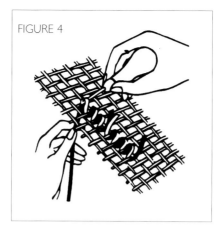

FIGURE 4

HOW TO HOOK

These basic instructions apply to hooking with all widths of woolen strips. Step 3, however, applies to hooking with narrow strips in #3, 4, and 5 cuts. (The number refers to the numerical designation of a cutter wheel on a fabric cutting machine. A #3 wheel cuts a strip $^3/_{32}$" wide; a #5 cuts a strip $^5/_{32}$" wide; a #8, $^8/_{32}$" or $^1/_4$" wide, and so on.) Refer to the section on hooking with wide strips for special tips on holding a hook when making a wide-cut rug.

1 Stretch the backing in a hoop or frame with the design side up. Sitting comfortably, rest the hoop or frame on a table or your lap. The thumbscrew of a hoop should be opposite you.

2 With your left hand (right hand if you're a leftie) hold the end of a woolen strand between your thumb and forefinger (Figure 3).

3 With your right hand, hold the hook as if it were a pencil, with your fingertips on the metal collar as shown.

4 Hold the wool in your left hand and put it beneath the backing. With your right hand, push the hook down through the mesh. The shaft of the hook should

touch your left forefinger and slide behind the woolen strip. Push the wool onto the barb with your left thumb.

5 With the hook, pull the end of the strip through to the front of the backing, to a height of about $^1/_2$".

6 Push the hook down through the backing a little to the left of the strip's end and catch the strip underneath. Pull up a $^1/_8$" loop, or as high as the strip is wide. To prevent pulling out the previous loop, lean the hook back toward the previous loop as you pull up another loop.

7 Working from right to left, make even loops that gently touch each other as in Figure 4. With fine strips, hook in almost every hole. Never put more than one loop in a hole.

8 When you reach the end of the woolen strip, pull the end up through the backing. Pull all ends through to the front as you hook. Tails on the back are untidy and can be easily pulled out.

9 Start the next strip in the same hole in which the last strip ended, again leaving a $^1/_2$" tail.

10 Trim the ends even with the loops after making several loops with the new strip.

11 Continue the hooking process until the pattern is complete. To

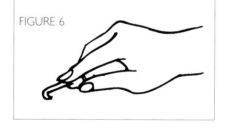

FIGURE 6

FIGURE 5

keep the back of the rug from becoming lumpy, do not cross a row of hooking with another strip. Cut the strip and start again.

12 Practice the following exercises to achieve the proper rhythm and technique: (a) after hooking straight lines, try wavy lines; (b) pack rows against one another to form a pile as in Figure 5.

Even the most skilled rug hooker must pull out loops now and then. Individual strands can be removed easily, but loops in packed areas are harder to remove. Use the hook or a pair of tweezers. Strands may be re-used if they are not badly frayed, and the blank area of the backing may be hooked again.

HOOKING WITH WIDE STRIPS

When hooking with wide strips ($1/4$" to $1/2$"), note that they pull up more easily if you hold the hook in the palm of your hand (Figure 6) and insert it into the backing at a sharper angle. (Some even prefer to hold the hook in this manner when working with narrow strips.) As with narrow strips, the shaft of the hook should rub the forefinger of your left hand and pass behind the woolen strip. The barb should hit your thumb, which pushes the wool onto the hook. Never loop the wool over the hook with your left hand; this will result in a lumpy back. If you cannot pick up the strip with your hook, the barb is not properly positioned.

—Happy and Steve DiFranza

General Quilting Directions

Read through the pattern directions before purchasing fabric for the quilt. Wash fabrics in the manner in which you intend to wash the finished quilt. This preshrinks the fabrics and ensures that they are colorfast. Dry fabric and press to remove wrinkles.

Most fabrics are sold as 44" wide, but many vary slightly in width. Fabric width may also change after the fabric is washed. The fabric lists and cutting directions in the book are based on fabric that is at least 42" wide after washing.

Backing fabric and batting dimensions listed in the pattern are for hand quilting or for quilting on a home sewing machine. Professional quilters using a long-arm machine may require a larger backing and batting size. If you intend to have someone else quilt your project,

consult them regarding backing and backing size. Cut backing fabric and sew pieces together as necessary to achieve the desired size.

TEMPLATES

The template patterns provided for pieced quilts are full size with an included $1/4$" seam allowance. A seam allowance is not included on appliqué template patterns. Trace template patterns, including any grainline arrows, onto your template material.

MARKING FABRIC PIECES

Test marking pens and pencils for removability before marking pieces for your quilt. If the pattern piece includes a grainline arrow, align the arrow with the fabric

grain. Use your marker to trace around the template on the right side of the fabric, then cut the pieces out.

If you wish to mark the sewing line, use a quilter's $1/4$" ruler to measure and mark the seam allowance on the wrong side of the fabric. Mark the pieces needed to complete one block, cut them out, and stitch them together before cutting pieces for the entire quilt.

Trace appliqué templates lightly on the right side of the fabric. Add the seam allowance specified in the pattern when cutting the fabric pieces out.

PIECING

Set your sewing machine to sew 12 stitches per inch. If you have not marked the stitching line on fabric pieces, be careful to align fabric edges with the marks on the throat plate of your machine, as necessary, to achieve an accurate $1/4$" seam allowance. You can also make a stitching guide by placing a ruler under the presser foot of the sewing machine, aligning the $1/4$" marked line on the ruler with the needle. Align a piece of masking tape or a rectangle cut from a moleskin footpad along the right edge of the ruler. Remove the ruler, and place fabric edges against the stitching guide as you sew. Stitch fabric pieces from edge to edge unless directed otherwise in the pattern.

Sew fabric pieces together in the order specified in the pattern. Wherever possible, press seam allowances toward the darkest fabric. When butting seams, press seam allowances in opposing directions.

APPLIQUÉ

You can stitch appliqué pieces to the background fabric either by hand or by machine. For needle-turn appliqué, lightly trace the pattern pieces on the right side of the fabric and add a narrow turn-under allowance (seam allowance) when cutting the pieces out. Pin pieces to the background fabric and stitch them in place, beginning with the underlying pieces. If stitching by hand, use an appliqué needle to turn the seam allowance under as you stitch. Do not turn raw edges under if they will be covered by other appliqué pieces. If stitching by machine, use a blind-hem stitch or a blanket stitch along the folded edge. An alternative is to cut out the appliqué pieces on the marked line without adding a seam allowance and finish the edges by machine using a satin stitch.

FUSIBLE APPLIQUÉ

This method allows you to complete appliqué very quickly. Follow the directions on the fusible product to prepare and attach appliqué pieces. For most fusible products, it is necessary to flip asymmetrical templates right side down before tracing them on the paper side of the fusible web. Finish the edges of fused appliqué pieces by hand using a blanket stitch or by machine using either a blanket or satin stitch.

MARKING THE QUILT TOP

Press the quilt top. Test all markers for removability before using them on a quilt. If using a paper design, place it under the quilt top, and trace the design. Use a light source if necessary. If using a stencil, place it on top of the quilt top, and trace the open areas. Use a ruler to mark straight lines such as grids or diagonals that cross fabric pieces.

Masking tape can be used as an alternative to marking straight lines. Place the tape on the quilt where desired and stitch along the edge. Contact paper can be cut into strips and used in the same manner. It can also be cut into other quilting shapes or stencils. Remove tape and contact paper from the quilt top daily to avoid leaving a sticky residue on the quilt.

BASTING

To prepare a quilt for hand quilting, open up the batting and place it on a flat surface (a bed or carpeted area is ideal). Place the pressed backing fabric wrong side up on a flat, solid surface. Secure the backing in place with masking tape. Smooth the batting on top of the backing. Center the quilt top right side up on the batting.

Use a needle and thread in a color that contrasts with the quilt. Baste with large stitches, keeping all knots on top of the quilt. Begin in the quilt center and baste first horizontally, then vertically, and finally diagonally to the edge of the quilt top.

To prepare your quilt for quilting on your home sewing machine, use soluble thread to baste the quilt, or baste using safety pins.

QUILTING

Many fine books are available on both hand and machine quilting. Basic hand quilting is described here.

Use quilting thread and a short, strong needle. Place a thimble on the middle finger of your preferred hand. Always begin quilting in the center of the quilt and work your way toward the quilt edge. Make a small knot at the end of the thread, and insert the threaded needle into the quilt top and batting only near where you wish

QUILT	APPROXIMATE SIZE
Baby Quilt	36" x 54"
Lap Throw	54" x 72"
Twin	54" x 90"
Double	72" x 90"
Queen	90" x 108"
King	108" x 108"

your first quilting stitch to appear. Exit the needle at the beginning of where you want your first visible stitch to be and gently pop the knot between the fabric fibers into the quilt top.

Begin quilting as follows: Keeping your preferred hand above the quilt and your other hand below it, use your thimbled finger to push the needle straight down through all layers of the quilt. When you feel the tip of the needle with the index or middle finger of the hand underneath, use the thumb of your preferred hand to depress the quilt top, and redirect the needle back through the quilt layers to the top of the quilt. Continue in this manner using a rocking motion with your preferred hand. When the thread becomes short, make a small knot at the surface of the quilt top. Then take a stitch and pop the knot into the quilt. Cut the thread where it exits the quilt top. Do not remove basting stitches until quilting is complete.

BINDING STRIPS

Quilts with straight edges can be bound with binding strips cut with the grain of the fabric. Cut binding strips the width specified in the quilt pattern, and sew them together with diagonal seams in the following way: Place two binding strips right sides together and perpendicular to each other, aligning the ends. Mark a line on the top strip, from the upper left edge of the bottom strip to the lower right edge of the top strip, and stitch on the marked line. Trim the seam allowance $1/4$" beyond the stitching, open up the strips, and press the seam allowance open. When all binding strips have been stitched together, fold the strip in half lengthwise (wrong side in) and press.

ATTACHING THE BINDING

Leaving at least 6" of the binding strip free and beginning several inches away from a corner of the quilt top, align the raw edges of the binding with the edge of the quilt top. Using a standard $1/4$" seam allowance, stitch the binding to the quilt, stopping and backstitching exactly $1/4$" from the corner of the quilt top.

Remove the quilt from the sewing machine, turn the quilt so the stitched portion of the binding is away from you, and fold the binding away from the quilt, forming a 45-degree angle on the binding. *Hint: When the angle is correct, the unstitched binding strip will be aligned with the next edge of the quilt top.*

Maintaining the angled corner fold, fold the loose binding strip back down, aligning this fold with the stitched edge of the quilt top and the raw edge of the binding with the adjacent quilt top edge. Stitch the binding to the quilt beginning at the fold, backstitching to secure the seam.

Continue attaching the binding in the same manner until you arrive 6" from the first stitching. Then, fold both loose ends of the binding strip back upon themselves so that the folds meet in the center of the unstitched section of the binding, and crease the folds.

Measure the width of the folded binding strip. Cut both ends of the binding strip that measurement beyond the creased folds. (For example: If the quilt pattern instructed you to cut the binding strips $2^1/2$" wide, the folded binding strip would measure $1^1/4$". In this case, you would cut both ends of the binding strip $1^1/4$" beyond the creased folds.)

Open up both ends of the binding strip and place them right sides together and perpendicular to each other. Mark a line on the top strip from the upper left corner of the top strip to the lower right corner of the bottom strip. Pin the strips together and stitch on the marked line.

Refold the binding strip and place it against the quilt top to test the length. Open the binding strip back up, trim the seam allowance $1/4$" beyond the stitching, and finger press the seam allowance open. Refold the binding strip, align the raw edges with the edge of the quilt top, and finish stitching it to the quilt.

Trim the batting and backing $3/8$" beyond the binding stitching. Fold the binding to the back of the quilt and blind stitch it to the backing fabric covering the machine stitching. Keep your stitches small and close together. When you reach a corner, stitch the mitered binding closed on the back side of the quilt, and pass the needle through the quilt to the right side. Stitch the mitered binding closed on the front side of the quilt, and pass the needle back through the quilt to the back side. Continue stitching the folded edge of the binding to the back of the quilt.

FINISHING YOUR QUILT

Remove all quilt markings. Make a label that includes your name, the city where you live, the date the quilt was completed, and anything else you would like future owners of the quilt to know. Permanent fabric pens make this task easy and allow you to make the label as decorative as desired. Stitch the label to the back of the quilt.

Rug Hooking *Resources*

The following is a list of sources for the many materials and techniques discussed in this book. Keep in mind that this is only a partial list of the many companies that sell these products. Most of these companies, and many more, advertise in Rug Hooking *magazine. These companies can get you started with all the supplies needed to make hand-hooked rugs. The rest is up to you. Enjoy!*

American Folk Art & Craft Supply
604b Bedford St. (Rt. 18)
Abington, MA 02351
(781) 871-7277
www.americanfolkartonline.com
Made to order custom braided rugs, rug hooking supplies, and penny rug supplies and classes.

Beehive Hooking
Laura Schulze
3611 River Oaks Ct.
Tyler, TX 75707
(903) 566-4522
www.beehivehooking.com
All supplies for hooking rugs, kits, and finished rugs as well as a journal on the website.

Black Sheep Wool Designs
Rhonda and Marty Manley
(816) 781-6844
www.blacksheepwooldesigns.com
Featuring a full line of rug hooking supplies, patterns, and wool.

Bruce Grinding & Machining
PO Box 539
Bridgewater, NS B4V 2X6, Canada
(902) 543-7762
Bolivar cutting machines.

By the Door Hooked Rugs
Deanne Fitzpatrick
RR 5
19 Pumping Street Road
Amherst, NS, B4H 3Y3, Canada
www.hookingrugs.com
(800) 328-7756
Complete line of supplies, kits, and patterns.

Castle in the Clouds
7108 Panavista Lane
Chattanooga, TN 37421
(423) 892-1858
castlerug@comcast.net
www.geocities.com/castlerug
Fleecewood Farm Patterns, including Pumpkin Boy.

Cox Enterprises
10 Dube Road
Verona Island, ME 04416
(207) 469-6402
How-to videos and books on hooking and braiding for beginners and advanced crafters.

Cross Creek Farm Rug Studio and School
Burton, Ohio
Beth Croup
13440 Taylor Wells Road
Chardon, OH 44024
(440) 635-0209
Workshops and Katherine Porter patterns, By appointment only.

Dorr Mill Store
PO Box 88
Guild, NH 03754
(800) 846-3677
dorrmillstore@sugar-river.net
www.dorrmillstore.com
Quality wools, color palettes, patterns, kits, and much more.

Emma Lou's Hooked Rugs
Emma Lou Lais
8643 Hiawatha Road
Kansas City, MO 64114
(816) 444-1777
Primitive rug patterns.

Fredericksburg Rugs
15001 Walden Road, Suite 100
Montgomery, TX 77356
(800) 331-5213
www.fredericksburgrugs.com
fredrugs@consolidated.net
Complete rug hooking supplies, hand-dyed wool, wool by the yard, patterns.

Green Mountain Hooked Rugs
Stephanie Ashworth Krauss
146 Main Street
Montpelier, VT 05602
(802) 223-1333
www.GreenMountainHookedRugs.com
Patterns, supplies, and the annual Green Mountain Rug School.

Halcyon Yarn
12 School Street
Bath, ME 04530
(800) 341-0282
www.halcyonyarn.com
service@halcyonyarn.com
High-quality rug yarn for finishing hooked rugs.

Harry M. Fraser Company
433 Duggins Road
Stoneville, NC 27048
(336) 573-9830
fraserrugs@aol.com
www.fraserrugs.com
Cloth-slitting machines, hooking, and braiding supplies.

Hartman's Hooks
Cindy Hartman
PO Box 938
Hudson, OH 44236
(330) 603-0057
hhooks@mac.com
Hartman Hooks.

Heirloom Rugs
124 Tallwood Drive
Vernon, CT 06066
(860) 870-8905
www.heirloomrugs.com
heirloomrugs@aol.com
Supplier of Zeiser, Skatet and Hookraft Designs

Heritage Rug™ Hooking
13845 Magnolia Avenue
Chino, CA 91710
(909) 591-6351
www.mcgtextiles.com
Complete rug hooking and finishing supplies.

Hook Nook
Margaret Siano
1 Morgan Road
Flemington, NJ 08822
(908) 806-8083
www.hook-nook.com
Lib Callaway rug patterns, hooking supplies, and instructions.

Jane Olson Rug Studio
PO Box 351
Hawthorne, CA 90250
(310) 643-5902
(310) 643-7367 (fax)
www.janeolsonrugstudio.com
The total rug hooking and braiding supplier for 33 years.

London-Wul Fibre Arts
Heidi Wulfraat
1937 Melanson Road
Lakeburn, NB, E1H 2C6, Canada
(506) 382-6990
www.thewoolworks.com
Specialty yarns and fibers.

Morton Frames
311 Park Street
Winfield, KS 67156
(620) 221-1299
Country@kcisp.net
Rug hooking frames.

Patsy B
Patsy Becker
PO Box 1050
S. Orleans, MA 02662
(508) 240-0346
patsyb@c4.net
Over 250 primitive patterns.

PRO Chemical & Dye
PO Box 14
Somerset, MA 02726
(800) 228-9393
Fax: (508) 676-3908
www.prochemical.com
Dyeing supplies.

Pris Buttler Rug Designs
PO Box 591
Oakwood ,GA 30566-0010
(770) 718-0090
prisrugs@charter.net
Pris Buttler patterns, including Lamb's Tongues and Sunflowers.

Rigby Cutters
PO Box 158
249 Portland Road
Bridgeton, ME 04009
(207) 647-5679
Cloth stripping machines.

Ruckman Mill Farm
Susan Feller
PO Box 409
Augusta, WV 26704
(908) 832-9565
www.ruckmanmillfarm.com
Susan Feller's rug designs.

Spruce Top Rug Hooking Studio
255 West Main St.
Mahone Bay, NS, B0J 2E0, Canada
(888) RUG-HOOK
www.sprucetoprughookingstudio.com

The Wool Studio
706 Brownsville Road
Sinking Spring, PA 19608
(610) 678-5448
www.thewoolstudio.com
rebecca@thewoolstudio.com
Quality woolens, specializing in textures for the primitive rug hooker. Send $5 for swatches.

Woolley Fox, LLC
Barbara Carroll
132 Woolley Fox Lane
Ligonier, PA 15658
(724) 238-3004
www.woolleyfox.com
Primitive patterns, custom kits, Gingher scissors, and other supplies.

Woolrich Woolen Mill
Catalog Orders
Two Mill Street
Woolrich, PA 17779
(570) 769-6464
(Ask for Mill Sales, ext. 327)
rughooking@woolrich.com
Factory direct rug hooking wool.

Yankee Peddler
Marie Azzaro
267 Route 81
Killingworth, CT 06419
(860) 663-0526
Cutters, hand-dyed wool, hooks, and patterns, including Museum Bed Rug and Bed Rug Fantasy.